CHARACTERS RECREATED BY CAROL MELDRUM

SETS, PROPS AND MODELS RECREATED BY RUTH HERBERT

BASED ON THE CLANGERS FILMS MADE BY OLIVER POSTGATE AND PETER FIRMIN, AS SMALLFILMS, FOR THE BBC

Clangers

Make the Clangers
and their planet
with 15 easy
step-by-step projects

COLLINS & BROWN

CONTENTS

When the BBC asked in the mid-sixties for a new series of space-age puppet films for the younger audience, Oliver Postgate and I trawled through ten years' work to see what we could find.

As Smallfilms, we had produced films and books such as *Ivor the Engine*, *The Pogles* and *The Saga of Noggin the Nog*.

In one of the Noggin books, Oliver had caused a small object, rather like a teapot, to fall out of space and land with a big splash in the new horse-trough.

Out of this space-craft climbed a small mouse-like creature with a duffle-coat and a pig-tail. It was called a 'Moon-mouse'. After alarming adventures with the children, it was saved by Queen Nooka and sent back into space.

We decide to update this creature, discover where it lived and find out about its family and friends. We discovered a blue planet covered with craters with metal lids. Under these lids a family of knitted pink creatures called Clangers lived in their caves. Oliver and I made 26 films of their lives. We hope you will have as much fun making these puppets and models as Oliver, my wife Joan and I did.

A SMALL BLUE PLANET

A long way away in a far corner of the sky, on a clear night you can see a faint blue-coloured star. Well it isn't really a star, it's a planet, but it is such a small and unimportant planet that it doesn't have a name. For one family, however, it is a very important place. It is the home of the Clangers.

Clangers are not like any of the creatures that live on Earth. They look rather like long-nosed, bright pink mice. They wear armour plates or cloth pads as clothes and they stand upright on big flappy feet. They talk to each other with a kind of high-pitched whistling and have large animated ears that they pull over their eyes when they are sad or distressed.

Clangers get inside their planet through holes that are protected by stout metal lids. It is the cling-clang-clonk sound, which these lids make when they are slammed shut, that gives the Clangers their name.

Life for the Clangers is calm and peaceful and they only worry when things fall from the sky to interrupt this peace. Lots of things land on the Clangers' planet, such as the Iron Chicken that originally arrived in pieces (after a Clanger rocket hit it) and was reconstructed by the Clangers. Little wonder that the Clangers have stout metal lids to cover their holes.

In 1969, around the same time as NASA's moon landing, the Clangers featured in a BBC TV series, which many people remember with affection. Now, over forty years later, you can not

only make your own Clanger with the original knitting pattern, but you can also build a Clanger world of your own, complete with the Clangers' most important friends – the Soup-Dragon, the Iron Chicken and the Froglets.

We hope you are completely over-excited at the thought of entering the Clangers' world once again.

The best way of getting to know the Clangers is to introduce them one by one.

Major Clanger is the head of the family; he is the largest and oldest Clanger and he wears armour made from beaten brass, but he does not fight – his armour protects him from things that fall from the sky.

Mother Clanger looks after everyone. Like all mothers, she is kind and loving, but sometimes cross when her son, Small Clanger, falls in a soup well, and her daughter, Tiny Clanger, tangles herself up in blue-string pudding.

Small Clanger and Tiny Clanger spend a lot of time playing and exploring, and Small Clanger loves to experiment with all sorts of things.

Grannie Clanger lives in a cave under the path and is forever knitting with frost-wool.

She lives a quiet life in her little cave and likes to collect the silver threads of frost that

catch on the edges of the craters and knit them into tinsel string.

The Clanger family share their world with various strange but friendly characters. The most important is the Soup-Dragon, who lives inside the planet and cooks soup (the Clangers' favourite food) in the volcanic wells that lie beneath the planet's surface.

Another friend, the Iron Chicken, lives somewhere in space on her cosy, comfy, spiky nest of old scrap-iron and bits of machinery that she has gathered up in her travels.

Then there are the Froglets, who live in a lake of pink soup in a cave at the middle of the planet. They are rather odd creatures, but like the Clangers they are quite ordinary and reasonable when you get used to them.

MOON SURFACE

WHAT YOU NEED

- Four 2-litre plastic milk bottles (or other washed empty plastic bottles), with lids screwed on
- Four cereal boxes (the same size)
- Newspapers (to pack the cereal boxes and to make papier-mâché)
- Glue
- Home-made glue (see page 94)
- Scissors
- Pencil
- Ruler
- Small piece of thin card
- Three lids off glass jars or yoghurt pots (approx. 7 cm in diameter)
- Silver spray paint
- Acrylic or poster paints (light and dark blues, and white)
- Paintbrush

On Earth human beings spend time outdoors and indoors; similarly, the Clangers enjoy their blue-cratered planet from the outside and the inside.

1. Firstly place an empty plastic bottle in each cereal box, then fill the gaps with scrunched-up newspaper. Make sure they are padded out quite firmly to strengthen the set. Stick down the tops of the boxes. Then using the diagram as reference, stick the four boxes together.

2. Follow the instructions on page 94 to make the home-made glue. Cut up some newspapers, firstly into pieces measuring 15 × 15 cm. With your finger, dot a little glue onto the newspaper pieces and start to layer them over the joins of the set. This is the best way to get rid of the joins between the cardboard boxes, without making the set too wet. If the set gets too wet, it can take a long time to dry out and can start to go mouldy.

3. Now cut up some more newspaper, this time into 3 × 3 cm pieces. Dip them one by one in the bowl of glue and, using your fingers, wipe off any excess glue. With these smaller gluey pieces, start covering the dry pieces of newspaper on the joins. After covering the joins, continue to cover the rest of the set with papier-mâché (see page 94).

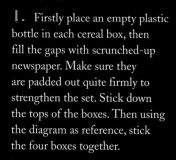

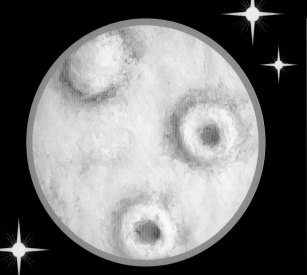

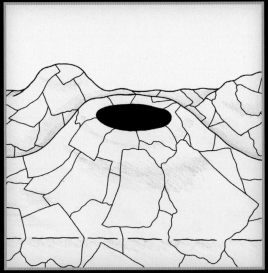

Meteorites and odd bits of rock and other, even odder, things often come down with a bump on the outside of the Clangers' planet.

No wonder the Clangers have stout metal lids to cover their holes.

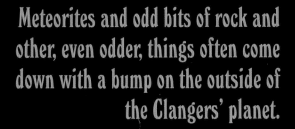

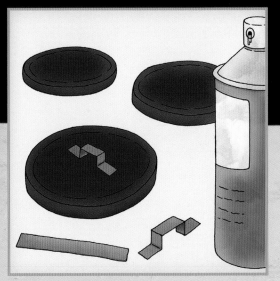

4. To make a moon crater, twist a long thin piece of newspaper and curl it into a circle: the diameter should be approximately 7 cm. Dab a little glue on the crater and stick it on the moon surface. Cut up some newspaper into 7 cm × 10 cm pieces, dip them in the home-made glue and cover the crater so that it blends into the moon surface. The finished diameter of the crater should be approximately 10 cm at the widest point. Repeat this process to make two more craters.

5. For the moon mound, roll some newspaper into a small ball. Dab a little glue onto the ball and stick it on the moon surface. Cover the mound with papier-mâché so that it becomes part of the moon surface.

6. Put the set in a warm place to dry. Once it is dry, check if any of the joins between the cardboard boxes are showing. If they are, add a few more layers of papier-mâché to neaten the look of the set. You may wish to neaten the craters and mound in the same way.

7. For the moon crater lids, firstly, draw three lid handles on thin card, each one measuring 44 × 6 mm. Cut out, score and bend them as in the diagram. Glue one handle onto each jar or yoghurt pot lid, and spray them silver.

8. Once the moon surface is finished and completely dry, paint it using a palette of blue and white paints to get a variety of shades. Lastly, place the moon lids on top of the craters and the set is ready for you to add music trees, a rocket or a boat.

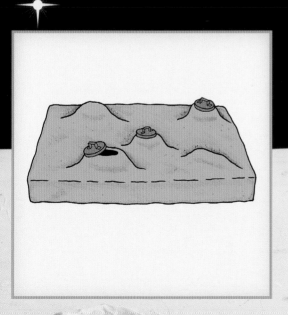

TINY CLANGER

Clangers are very clever at making things.

FINISHED SIZE
Approx. 12 cm to top of head

YARN
50-g ball of Rowan Pure Wool DK in Tea Rose 025

MATERIALS
- Pair of 2.75-mm knitting needles
- Yarn or tapestry needle and safety pins for sewing up
- Toy stuffing
- Pins
- Oddment of black felt for eyes and feet
- Sewing needle and thread to match each colour of felt
- Oddment of pink felt for nose, ears and hands
- Thin card
- Oddment of felt for hair in colour of your choice
- Sheet of red felt for tunic, approx. 23 × 30 cm
- Small amount of metallic gold thread or 4-ply yarn for tunic embroidery
- Oddment of orange felt for bow

TENSION
Approx. 32 sts and 45 rows to 10 cm over stocking stitch using 2.75-mm needles

ABBREVIATIONS
See page 81

TEMPLATES
See pages 82–83

HEAD, BODY AND LEGS

Cast on 6 sts.

Row 1 (RS): Knit.

Row 2: Purl.

Repeat last two rows once more.

Row 5: K1, m1, k to last st, m1, k1. (8 sts)

Row 6: Purl.

Repeat last two rows until there are 18 sts, ending with a purl row.

Row 17: As row 5. (20 sts)

Row 18: P1, m1, p to last st, m1, p1. (22 sts)

Repeat last two rows until there are 28 sts, ending with a knit row.

Row 22: Purl.

SHAPE BACK OF HEAD

Next row (RS): K1, m1, k to last 2 sts, turn.

Next row: Sl1, p to last 2 sts, turn.

Next row: Sl1, k to last 4 sts, turn.

Next row: Sl1, p to last 4 sts, turn.

Continue in this way, working 2 sts less on each row until 'sl1, p to last 12 sts, turn' has been worked.

Next row: Sl1, k to last st, m1, k1. (30 sts)

Next row: Purl to end.

Continue working in stocking stitch, increasing 1 st as set in row 5 at each end of every knit row until there are 42 sts, ending with a knit row.

SHAPE ARMHOLES

Next row (WS): P8, cast off next 4 sts, p18 (include st used in cast-off), cast off next 4 sts, p to end.

Next row: K1, m1, k7, turn, cast on 4 sts, turn, k18, turn, cast on 4 sts, turn, k to last st, m1, k1. (44 sts)

Next row: Purl to end.

Continue working in stocking stitch, increasing 1 st as set in row 5 at each end of every knit row until there are 48 sts.

Work next thirteen rows straight, ending with a purl row.

SHAPE LOWER BACK AND LEGS

Row 1 (RS): K8, k2tog, k4, k2tog, k16, k2tog tbl, k4, k2tog tbl, k to end. (44 sts)

Row 2 and all WS rows: Purl.

Row 3: K8, k2tog, k3, k2tog, k14, k2tog tbl, k3, k2tog tbl, k to end. (40 sts)

Row 5: K8, k2tog, k2, k2tog, k12, k2tog tbl, k2, k2tog tbl, k to end. (36 sts)

Row 7: Cast off 4 sts, k10 (include st used in cast-off), cast off 8 sts, k to end.

Row 8: Cast off 4 sts, p10 (include st used in cast-off), turn.

Starting with a knit row, work three rows in stocking stitch on this set of 10 sts.

Cast off and break off yarn.

With wrong side facing, rejoin yarn to remaining 10 sts and, starting with a purl row, work four rows in stocking stitch.

Cast off.

ARMS (MAKE 2)

Cast on 8 sts.

Row 1 (RS): Knit.

Row 2: Purl.

Row 3: K1, m1, k to last st, m1, k1. (10 sts)

Starting with a purl row, work three rows in stocking stitch.

Row 7: As row 3. (12 sts)

Starting with a purl row, work three rows in stocking stitch. Cast off.

OUTER EARS (MAKE 2)

Cast on 3 sts.

Row 1 (WS): Purl.

Row 2: K1, m1, k1, m1, k1. (5 sts)

Row 3: P1, m1, p3, m1, p1. (7 sts)

Starting with a knit row, work four rows in stocking stitch.

Row 8: K1, k2tog tbl, k1, k2tog, k1. (5 sts)

Row 9: Purl.

Row 10: K1, sl1, k2tog, psso, k1. (3 sts)

Cast off.

MAKING UP

Sew in all loose ends. Gently press arms and ears, and the outer edges of body to stop the edges from curling: this will help with the sewing up. Fold body in half, wrong sides together, and pin the edges at regular intervals to keep them even. With right side facing, use mattress stitch to sew from the bottom seam towards the nose. Starting from the cast-off edge, sew up the legs using a long enough tail of yarn so that you can sew the bottom seam once the Clanger has been stuffed. Insert stuffing through the open bottom seam, using a small amount to start with so that you do not overstuff the nose. Once stuffed, sew up the bottom seam. Fold one arm in half,

wrong sides together. With right side facing, use mattress stitch to sew up the cast-on edge and side seam of arm. Repeat for the second arm, then stuff both firmly and sew securely to the armholes.

FEATURES

To use the templates provided, trace the shapes and then cut them out from thin card or paper. Refer to the photographs as a guide for positioning the features and sew them in place using thread to match the felt colour.

Eyes: Cut two small circles of black felt, then pin and stitch to head.

Nose: Cut a small circle of pink felt, then stitch into position.

Ears: Using template and pink felt, cut two inner ears and stitch to wrong side of knitted outer ears. Pin and stitch ears to head, leaving enough space between the ears for the hair.

Hands: Using template and pink felt, cut two hands, then pin and stitch to bottom of arms.

Feet: Using template, cut four feet from black felt and two more from card. Trim the card pieces so that they are slightly smaller than the felt pieces. Sandwich each card piece between two black felt pieces and sew around the edges. Once both feet have been completed, pin and stitch to bottom of legs.

Hair: Using template, cut hair from desired colour of felt, then pin and stitch into position between ears.

OUTFIT

To use the templates provided, trace the shapes and then cut them out from thin card or paper. Refer to the photographs as a guide for making up the outfit.

Tunic: Using templates, cut the pieces for the tunic from red felt. Use metallic gold thread or 4-ply yarn to work a running stitch around the outer edges of each felt piece. Sew the tunic pieces together using red thread, checking regularly to make sure that the tunic will fit onto the body and the pieces are not too close together or too far apart.

Bow: Cut a rectangle of orange felt, approx. 2 × 2.5 cm. Pinch the felt at the centre to form a concertina shape, allowing the edges to fan out. Using orange thread, sew along the centre to secure. Position the bow on top of the head between the ears and sew to the hair.

You have to be quick to catch things in space and Tiny Clanger is very quick.

TINY CLANGER

MUSIC BOAT

WHAT YOU NEED

- Scalpel or craft knife with sharp blade
- Ruler
- Scissors
- Sheet of craft foam
- Thin card (or cereal box)
- Two pencils
- Black fine liner marker pen
- Red fine liner marker pen
- Green fine liner marker pen
- Hole punch
- Glue
- Black acrylic paint
- White acrylic paint
- Glue gun with glue sticks
- Cotton reel
- Two wooden barbeque skewers
- Gold spray paint

Tiny Clanger loves to sit in the music boat with her rod and magnet, waiting to cast for anything that comes by.

MAKING THE BOAT

1. Firstly photocopy the templates on pages 84–85, enlarging them by the amount stated. Using the scalpel and ruler or scissors, carefully cut out the templates.

2. Place template 9 on the craft foam, cut it out and put it to one side. Place the rest of the templates on the thin card and draw around them. Take off the templates and, using the scalpel and ruler or scissors, cut them out. Make sure to label them. (See tips for using templates on page 82.)

3. Using the pencil and ruler, copy all the black lines onto the cut-outs. Then, using the red and green marker pens, copy all the red and green lines. Cut along the black lines, and score along the red lines using the back of the craft knife and the ruler. Carefully punch or cut out the holes in piece 2 – one for the mast and one for the rudder. Also punch or cut out the holes in pieces 7c and 8.

4. Take piece 1 (back) and fold over the tabs at the top and bottom along the red score lines. The smaller tabs are at the top of the boat and the larger tabs are at the bottom of the boat.

5. Now glue pieces 1 (back) and 2 (top) together. Bend piece 1 into a horseshoe shape and line up the green centre line with the green centre line on piece 2. Starting at the centre line, bit by bit glue the tabs around the curve at the back of the boat. Next glue piece 3 (base) to the larger tabs, starting at the centre, as before, and continuing around the curve.

6. Next make up the sides. Take piece 4a and fold it along the two red score lines. These two flaps should fit inside the top and base of the boat. The flap that has not been scored and folded should fit inside the curved back. Glue all the flaps and put 4a in place (see diagram). Repeat this step for the other side pieces 4b, 4c and 4d. If any of the pieces do not fit together correctly, you may need to trim them down.

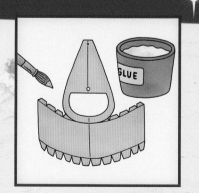

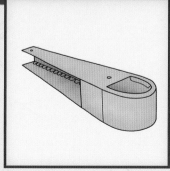

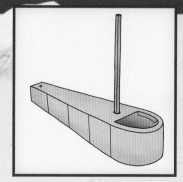

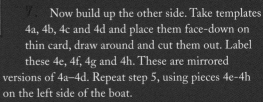

7. Now build up the other side. Take templates 4a, 4b, 4c and 4d and place them face-down on thin card, draw around and cut them out. Label these 4e, 4f, 4g and 4h. These are mirrored versions of 4a–4d. Repeat step 5, using pieces 4e-4h on the left side of the boat.

8. Glue piece 5 (nose) to the end of the boat. The main structure of the boat is now made.

9. With the scalpel or craft knife, chop off the sharpened end of one of the pencils. Slot the other, flat end of the pencil through the hole in the top of the boat (piece 2 - see page 21). This is the hole near to where Tiny Clanger sits. Push the pencil 1 mm through the hole so that it sits up vertically. To hold it in place, take the circular cut out piece 6, put a blob of

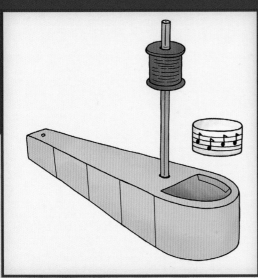

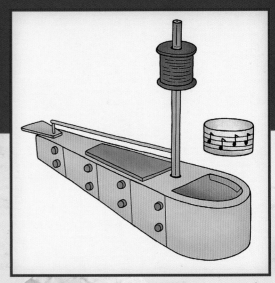

glue on one side, and put it underneath the top of the boat where the pencil sticks through the hole. Make sure the pencil sits at the right angle.

10. To make the music wheel and the mast for the boat, paint one side of 7a, 7b and 7c white. Once 7a has dried, using the pencil carefully measure and draw on the four lines of the staves. Draw over them with the black fine liner. Now draw on the music notes with the pencil and then colour them in with the black fine liner.

11. Fold over all the tabs (top and bottom) of 7a and bend it into a cylinder. Now glue 7a (the cylinder) to 7b (top of music wheel). Glue the tabs bit by bit until you have glued 7a right around the circumference of 7b (see diagram.) Do the same with 7c (bottom of music wheel), to create the final piece.

12. Slide the music wheel over the top of the pencil. Draw a line around the pencil where the music wheel stops: this should be 3 cm from the end of the pencil. Take off the music wheel and put to one side.

13. Hot glue all the way around the pencil just below the drawn line and quickly push the cotton reel down, so the top of the cotton reel is level with the top of the pencil line.

14. With the scalpel or craft knife, cut a piece of skewer 4 cm long and push it through the small hole at the end of the boat so it touches the base. Make sure that it is vertically parallel with the pencil. Put small blobs of hot glue around the skewer where it is poking out of the hole. Do this slowly, so that the glue has time to cool and harden, and until it is a hardened lump 5 mm high on the top of the boat. This will create a tiny gap between the boat and the wing (piece 8).

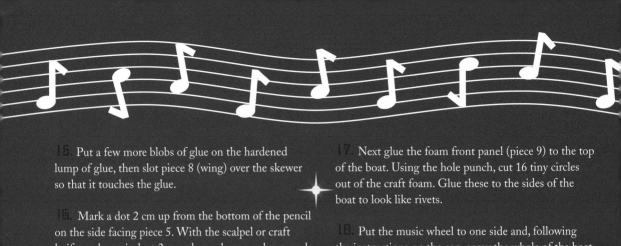

15. Put a few more blobs of glue on the hardened lump of glue, then slot piece 8 (wing) over the skewer so that it touches the glue.

16. Mark a dot 2 cm up from the bottom of the pencil on the side facing piece 5. With the scalpel or craft knife, make an indent 2 mm deep where you have made this mark. Now cut a skewer to 16 cm long: this should fit between the pencil and the top of the skewer with piece 8 attached. Hot glue both ends in place.

17. Next glue the foam front panel (piece 9) to the top of the boat. Using the hole punch, cut 16 tiny circles out of the craft foam. Glue these to the sides of the boat to look like rivets.

18. Put the music wheel to one side and, following the instructions on the can, spray the whole of the boat gold. It is much better to give the boat a thin layer of paint, leave this to dry then repeat the process a couple of times. This will ensure that the coat is even and that it does not run.

19. Once the gold paint is completely dry, glue the music wheel to the top of the cotton reel and the boat is ready.

WHAT YOU NEED

- Scalpel or craft knife with sharp blade
- Thick card
- Silver spray paint
- Masking tape
- Red acrylic paint
- Paintbrush
- Craft wire
- Pliers
- One wooden barbeque skewer
- One small bead
- Glue
- Gold spray paint
- White sewing thread

MAKING TINY'S FISHING ROD

1. Cut a magnet shape out of card. Spray the ends silver, using masking tape to cover the rest. When dry, remove the tape and paint the rest of the magnet red. Leave to dry. Make a small hole in the top centre of the magnet.

2. Cut three 3-cm lengths of craft wire. Twist each piece to form a loop and attach to the wooden skewer at intervals with masking tape; see photograph for position.

3. Take the bead and squirt a little glue inside it. Quickly thread it onto the wooden skewer, sliding it so that it sits about 4 cm from the end. Once the glue has dried, spray the fishing rod gold. Leave to dry.

4. Pass sewing thread through the hole in the magnet, through the wire loops and tie it under the bead. Use glue to secure the knot, then trim excess thread.

SMALL CLANGER

FINISHED SIZE
Approx. 16 cm to top of head

YARN
50-g ball of Rowan Pure Wool DK in Tea Rose 025

MATERIALS
- Pair of 2.75-mm knitting needles
- Yarn or tapestry needle and safety pins for sewing up
- Toy stuffing
- Pins
- Oddment of black felt for eyes and feet
- Oddment of pink felt for nose, ears and hands
- Sewing needle and thread to match each colour of felt
- Thin card
- Oddment of felt for hair in colour of your choice
- Sheet of beige felt for tunic, approx. 23 × 30 cm
- Gold craft paint
- Small paintbrush
- Small amount of 0.3-mm gold craft wire for sewing tunic
- 15 cm of 1-mm brass craft wire for collar
- Long-nose pliers

TENSION
Approx. 32 sts and 45 rows to 10 cm over stocking stitch using 2.75-mm needles

ABBREVIATIONS
See page 81

TEMPLATES
See pages 82–83

HEAD, BODY AND LEGS
Cast on 8 sts.
Row 1 (RS): Knit.
Row 2: Purl.
Repeat last two rows once more.
Row 5: K1, m1, k to last st, m1, k1. (10 sts)
Row 6: Purl.
Repeat last two rows until there are 24 sts, ending with a purl row.
Row 21: As row 5. (26 sts)
Row 22: P1, m1, p to last st, m1, p1. (28 sts)
Repeat last two rows until there are 36 sts, ending with a purl row.

SHAPE BACK OF HEAD

Next row (RS): K1, m1, k to last 2 sts, turn.

Next row: Sl1, p to last 2 sts, turn.

Next row: Sl1, k to last 4 sts, turn.

Next row: Sl1, p to last 4 sts, turn.

Continue in this way, working 2 sts less on each row until 'sl1, p to last 16 sts, turn' has been worked.

Next row: Sl1, k to last st, m1, k1. (38 sts)

Next row: Purl to end.

Continue working in stocking stitch, increasing 1 st as set in row 5 at each end of every knit row until there are 52 sts, ending with a knit row.

SHAPE ARMHOLES

Next row (WS): P10, cast off next 5 sts, p22 (include st used in cast-off), cast off next 5 sts, p to end.

Next row: K1, m1, k9, turn, cast on 5 sts, turn, k22, turn, cast on 5 sts, turn, k to last st, m1, k1. (54 sts)

Next row: Purl to end.

Continue working in stocking stitch, increasing 1 st as set in row 5 at each end of next row. (56 sts) Work next fifteen rows straight, ending with a purl row.

SHAPE LOWER BACK AND LEGS

Row 1 (RS): K12, k2tog, k5, k2tog, k14, k2tog tbl, k5, k2tog tbl, k to end. (52 sts)

Row 2 and all WS rows: Purl.

Row 3: K12, k2tog, k4, k2tog, k12, k2tog tbl, k4, k2tog tbl, k to end. (48 sts)

Row 5: K12, k2tog, k3, k2tog, k10, k2tog tbl, k3, k2tog tbl, k to end. (44 sts)

Row 7: Cast off 5 sts, k12 (include st used in cast-off), cast off 10 sts, k to end.

Row 8: Cast off 5 sts, p12 (include st used in cast-off), turn.

Starting with a knit row, work six rows in stocking stitch on this set of 12 sts.

Cast off and break off yarn.

With wrong side facing, rejoin yarn to remaining 10 sts and, starting with a purl row, work seven rows in stocking stitch.

Cast off.

Small Clanger is notable for his experiments by which he learns and pushes back the boundaries of his world.

ARMS (MAKE 2)
Cast on 10 sts.
Row 1 (RS): Knit.
Row 2: Purl.
Row 3: K1, m1, k to last st, m1, k1.
  (12 sts)
Starting with a purl row, work four
rows in stocking stitch.
Row 8: P1, m1, p to last st, m1, p1.
  (14 sts)
Starting with a knit row, work four
rows in stocking stitch.
Cast off.

OUTER EARS (MAKE 2)
Cast on 4 sts.
Row 1 (WS): Purl.
Row 2: K1, m1, k2, m1, k1. (6 sts)
Row 3: Purl.

Row 4: K1, m1, k4, m1, k1. (8 sts)
Starting with a purl row, work
three rows in stocking stitch.
Row 8: K1, k2tog tbl, k2, k2tog,
  k1. (6 sts)
Row 9: Purl.
Row 10: K1, k2tog tbl, k2tog, k1.
  (4 sts)
Row 11: P1, p2tog, p1. (3 sts)
Cast off.

MAKING UP
Sew in all loose ends. Gently press
arms and ears, and the outer edges
of body to stop the edges from
curling: this will help with the
sewing up. Fold body in half, wrong
sides together, and pin the edges at
regular intervals to keep them even.
With right side facing, use
mattress stitch to sew from the
bottom seam towards the
nose. Starting from the
cast-off edge, sew up

the legs using a long enough tail
of yarn so that you can sew the
bottom seam once the Clanger
has been stuffed. Insert stuffing
through the open bottom seam,
using a small amount to start with
so that you do not overstuff the
nose. Once stuffed, sew up the
bottom seam. Fold one arm in half,
wrong sides together. With right
side facing, use mattress stitch to
sew up the cast-on edge and side
seam of arm. Repeat for the second
arm, then stuff both firmly and sew
securely to the armholes.

FEATURES
To use the templates provided, trace
the shapes and then cut them out
from thin card or paper. Refer to the
photographs as a guide for
positioning the features and sew
them in place using thread to match
the felt colour.

Eyes: Cut two small circles of black felt, then pin and stitch to head.

Nose: Cut a small circle of pink felt, then stitch into position.

Ears: Using template and pink felt, cut two inner ears and stitch to wrong side of knitted outer ears. Pin and stitch ears to head, leaving enough space between the ears for the hair.

Hands: Using template and pink felt, cut two hands, then pin and stitch to bottom of arms.

Feet: Using template, cut four feet from black felt and two more from card. Trim the card pieces so that they are slightly smaller than the felt pieces. Sandwich each card piece between two black felt pieces and sew around the edges. Once both feet have been completed, pin and stitch to bottom of legs.

Hair: Using template, cut hair from desired colour of felt, then pin and stitch into position between ears.

OUTFIT

To use the templates provided, trace the shapes and then cut them out from thin card or paper. Refer to the photographs as a guide for making up the outfit.

Tunic: Using templates, cut the pieces for the tunic from beige felt. Cut out two large S shapes from beige felt and sew onto the centre of the front and back tunic panels using beige thread. Lay all the tunic pieces on top of a sheet of newspaper to protect the surface you are working on and paint the pieces with gold paint. Leave to dry (approx. 1 hour). If required, apply another coat of gold for a stronger colour and leave to dry again. Sew the tunic pieces together using gold wire, checking regularly to make sure that the tunic will fit onto the body and the pieces are not too close together or too far apart. The tunic hangs on a brass wire collar around the Clanger's neck. Bend the brass wire and place it around the Clanger's neck to check that it fits, trimming if necessary. Grip one end of the wire with long-nose pliers and wind the wire around to form a loop. Repeat at the other end of the wire. Check once again that the collar fits, then bend the ends slightly downwards to an angle of approx. 45 degrees. Place the collar around the Clanger's neck, then sew the front and back of the tunic to the collar using gold wire.

The Clangers put up the see-saw jumping set. Wham-bonk! Major Clanger jumped on the first see-saw. Wheep-bonk! Small Clanger was thrown up and landed on the second see-saw. Wheep! Tiny Clanger was tossed high into the sky.

SEE-SAW

WHAT YOU NEED

- Scissors
- A5 piece of thick card
- Pencil
- Scalpel or craft knife with sharp blade
- Ruler
- Four wooden barbeque skewers
- Glue

1. Photocopy or trace the see-saw templates on page 86. Carefully cut them out and place them on the piece of card. Draw around, then take off the templates and cut out the shapes. You will need to cut out two of piece 2 (side of base) and two of piece 3 (the seat). Glue both sides (piece 2) to piece 1 as shown below, to make the base of the see-saw.

2. With the scalpel or craft knife, cut two lengths of skewer, each 24 cm long. Cut seven lengths of skewer, each 5 cm long. Lay the two long skewers parallel to each other, 5 cm apart. Glue a short length of skewer at each end and then mark five points along each skewer 4 cm apart. Glue the remaining short skewer pieces in place as shown in the diagram.

3. Once the 'ladder' is formed, glue the two seats (piece 3) at either end of the see-saw in place.

4. Spray paint both parts gold. Once the paint has dried, slot the top part into the grooves of the base and the see-saw is finished.

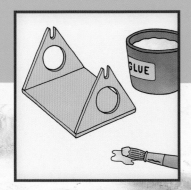

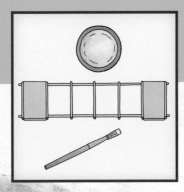

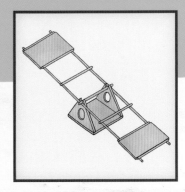

WHAT YOU NEED

- Scissors
- A4 piece of blue craft foam
- Fine liner
- Scalpel or craft knife with sharp blade
- A5 piece of thick card
- Blue acrylic paint
- Paintbrush
- Pins
- Orange fabric or felt, roughly 36 × 24 cm
- Needle and thread
- 3 cotton wool balls
- Glue
- Map pins

1. Photocopy the templates on page 87, enlarging them by the amount stated. Cut them out.

2. For the outside of the tree, place template 1 on the blue craft foam. Draw around it with the fine liner, and then carefully remove it. Turn the template over and, again, place it on the blue craft foam and draw around it. This should be a mirror image of the first template.

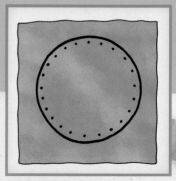

Cut out both trees. Use a sharp scalpel or craft knife for a clean cut.

3. For the inner structure of the pin tree, place templates 2 and 3 on a piece of thick card. Draw around them and cut them out. It is quite tricky cutting curved shapes in thick card, so use a sharp scalpel or craft knife and be careful. Place template 3 on the card and cut out another rectangle (label this 3a). Paint all three cutouts blue and leave to dry.

4. For the pincushions, poke holes through template 4 where the dots are. You will use the template five times, so be careful with it. Pin the template to the piece of orange fabric or felt. Draw around it with the fine liner, poking the pen through the small holes to mark

them. Take the template off and repeat four more times. Cut out the five orange circles.

5. Thread the needle with cotton and attach to one of the orange dots. Loosely stitch around the circle in and out of the dots. Break a cotton wool ball in half and place it in the centre of the orange fabric. Pull the thread tight to make a mini pincushion. Make four more mini pincushions.

6. Glue the inner tree cutout to the base cutouts 3 and 3a, following the diagram. Then take both outside tree cutouts (1) and, making sure that the sides of the foam with pen lines are both facing inwards, glue one either side of the tree's inner card structure. Glue the five pincushions onto the tree.

7. Next, glue the tree bases to the set (or a piece of cardboard). Hide these supporting flaps by covering them with papier-mâché (see page 94). Once this is dry, paint over the papier-mâché and put map pins into the pincushions.

Pin trees grow inside the caves. Mother Clanger sometimes gets cross when Small Clanger drops pin tree seeds in the bed caves and makes them prickly.

THE FROGLETS

1. First, paint the six eyes and three bodies, using a fine paintbrush and orange acrylic paint. Lay some newspaper on the work surface, as a protective cover. Place a small bead on the end of the knitting needle or a pencil. Hold the knitting needle in one hand, paint around the bead and leave to dry. Add another coat of paint, if required, until you are happy with the depth of colour. **Tip** Place the knitting needle in a tall glass so that the bead is not touching any surface while it dries.

2. Paint the other eyes and the oval beads for the bodies in the same way. Then using the black fine liner pen, draw a smile on each oval bead.

3. To work on the eyes, place a blob of Blu-Tack on the newspaper (to hold the bead in place) and put an eye bead on top, with the centre hole facing upward. Using the pencil, carefully draw a circle approximately 5 mm outside from the centre hole. Then carefully fill in

The Froglets live in a sideways lake of pink soup in the middle of the planet.

the pencilled circle with white acrylic paint to create the eye ball – leave to dry (see diagram A, below).

4. Next, paint a black circle in the centre of the white circle (see B below). When this is dry, using the black fine liner pen, draw a line approximately 1 mm outside the black centre circle (see C below). Insert a small piece of black felt into the centre hole of the eye bead (see D below), and then take the bead off the Blu-Tack and fill the other end of the hole with a piece of orange felt.

5. Cut the false eyelashes into six equal sections. Replace the painted eye bead on the blob of Blu-Tack with the eyeball facing forward. Carefully run some glue along the base of a piece of false eyelashes. Then place the lashes in position at the top of the white of the eye – an old knitting needle or cocktail stick will help you do this – and leave to dry. Once the eyelashes have been attached, trim them with the scissors to the required length. Repeat steps 3–5 for all six eyes.

6. To attach the eyes to the body, set the oval body bead vertically on a blob of Blu-Tack. Using instant glue, place a small dot of glue at the base of an eye, then carefully set into position at the top of oval bead – use the diagram as a guide. Repeat for the other eyes.

7. To make the feet, using the template on page 88 as a guide, cut out four feet from cardboard for each froglet. Paint one surface of each foot with black acrylic paint. Once they are dry, using the point of the knitting needle (or the point of a compass), pierce a hole for the leg to sit in towards the back of two of the pieces of cardboard.

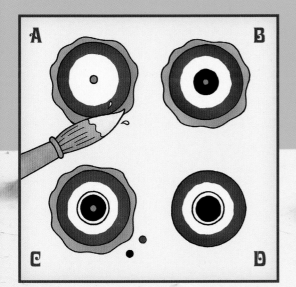

8. Next, glue the unpainted surfaces of the feet together. Once they are dry, paint around the edges of the feet and leave those to dry.

9. To make the legs, cut the barbeque skewer into six sections, approximately 2.5 cm long. Sand down any rough edges gently with the fine-grain sandpaper.

10. Put a large blob of Blu-Tack on the newspaper and place a section of leg in the centre. Paint the leg with black acrylic paint and leave to dry. Once dry, remove from the Blu-Tack and paint the unpainted end, then leave to dry. Once all the legs have been painted and are dry, place a small amount of glue in the hole in the top section each foot, insert a leg and leave to dry.

11. To attach the body to the legs, put the feet in pairs; make sure they are close together. Add a small dot of instant glue to the top of the legs, place the body gently on top of the legs, then hold until dry.

12. For the tail, using the template on page 88, cut out three tail shapes from orange felt. Place these on newspaper and paint them with orange acrylic paint to match the body, then leave to dry. Run a small amount of glue along the flat edge of the tail and, using the diagram as a guide, stick in position at the back of the froglet's body. Repeat steps 11 and 12 for the other two froglets.

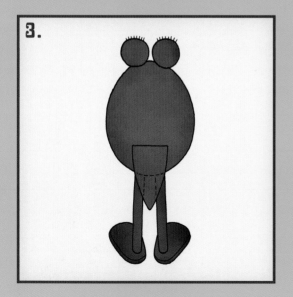

3.

Aark-plonk!
Up hopped a froglet.

Wheep-bonk!
Up out of a lid-hole
came their top hat.

Up came two more froglets who
danced croaking around the hat.

TOP HAT

WHAT YOU NEED

- Scissors
- Thick cardboard
- Pencil
- Thin craft card
- Craft knife
- Ruler
- Double-sided tape
- Grey acrylic paint
- Mid-grey felt
- Grey needlecord fabric, approx. 50 x 50 cm
- Light grey felt
- Button, 1.5 cm in diameter
- Needle
- Grey sewing thread

1. Photocopy the templates on page 88, enlarging them as stated. Carefully cut out the templates.

2. Place the top template on the thick card, draw around and cut it out. Next, cut out another top piece from thin craft card. Then cut out two brim pieces from thick cardboard.

3. Place the crown template on the thin craft card, draw around and cut it out Using the ruler and scissors, score along the red lines with the back of the craft knife and the ruler. Make short cuts down to the lines, about 1 cm apart, to make tabs. One row of tabs should bend inwards (the top ones) and the other row should bend outwards (the brim ones).

4. Bend the crown into a cylinder and secure the straight edges with a piece of double-sided sticky tape. Put some double-sided sticky tape around one of the cardboard brims. Put the crown on the brim, with the outwards bent tabs on the sticky tape. Press firmly to secure.

5. To attach the top to the crown, put double-sided sticky tape on the thick card top piece, then stick the inwards bent tabs of the crown to the tape. Put double-sided sticky tape on the wrong side of the thin card top, and stick it to the underside of the thick top, inside the crown, with the sticky side covering the tabs.

6. Add strips of double-sided sticky tape to the underside of the second brim piece. Slide it over the hat and press it down onto the first brim, sandwiching the tabs. Press firmly to secure. Paint the hat grey, or cover the brim with mid-grey felt and the crown and base with grey needlecord, using double-sided sticky tape. If you do use fabrics, you may find it easier to cover the top and crown before sticking the top on.

7. Cut out the bow pieces from the light grey felt. Fold piece 2 in half, and position in the centre of piece 1. Place piece 3 on top of piece 2, with the button on top, using the photograph as a guide. Sew all the pieces and button together. Place the light-grey strip around the hat just above the brim, making sure that the bow is at the front, and then sew the ends together.

MUSIC TREE

1. With the scalpel or craft knife, cut two cocktail sticks down to 4.5 cm, two to 4 cm and two to 3.5 cm. Then cut the skewer down to 15 cm. Following the diagram, glue the pieces together.

2. To make the music notes, use the pliers to cut twelve 3-cm lengths of black craft wire. Referring to the diagram and using the pliers, bend each piece of wire into a note shape about 15 mm high.

There are two music trees on the outside of the planet. Tiny Clanger successfully planted a couple of semiquavers, which the Soup-Dragon didn't eat. The trees make lots of music, which the Clangers enjoy; they also use the music to make their music boat fly.

3. Use the hole punch to cut twelve circles out of the black craft foam. Then cut out twelve strips of craft foam, each measuring 2 × 6 mm. Glue a circle and strip of craft foam to each wire note. Now glue the notes onto the tree.

4. To position the tree in the set, make a small hole in the set, put a blob of glue in the hole, and poke in the music tree. You can make a second tree in the same way.

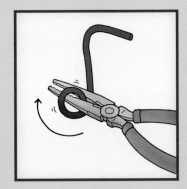

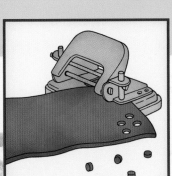

SOUP-DRAGON

FINISHED SIZE

Approx. 28 cm from nose to tail

YARN

Two 50-g balls of Rowan Pure Wool DK in Parsley 020

MATERIALS

- Pair of 3.25-mm knitting needles
- Two stitch holders (or spare knitting needles)
- Glass-headed pins for blocking
- Yarn or tapestry needle and safety pins for sewing up
- Toy stuffing
- 15-mm light blue teddy bear eyes on loop
- Thin card or paper for templates
- Sheet of felt, approx. 23 × 30 cm, in each of black, lime-green and dark green
- Oddment of felt in pink (tongue), turquoise (nostrils) and brown (spoon)
- Sewing needle
- Sewing thread in pink, black, green, turquoise and brown
- Thick cardboard for feet and spoon
- Sheet of green craft foam, approx. 23 × 30 cm

TENSION

Approx. 25 sts and 32 rows to 10 cm over stocking stitch using 3.25-mm needles

ABBREVIATIONS

See page 81

TEMPLATES

See page 89

UNDERBELLY

Cast on 9 sts.
Row 1 (RS): Knit.
Row 2: Purl.
Row 3: K1, m1, k to last st, m1, k1. (11 sts)
Row 4: P1, m1, p to last st, m1, p1. (13 sts)
Starting with a knit row, work ten rows in stocking stitch.
Row 15: K1, k2tog tbl, k to last 3 sts, k2tog, k1. (11 sts)
Starting with a purl row, work thirteen rows in stocking stitch.
Row 29: As row 3. (13 sts)
Row 30: Purl.
Repeat last two rows three more times. (19 sts)
Starting with a knit row, work eight rows in stocking stitch.
Row 45: As row 3. (21 sts)
Starting with a purl row, work five rows in stocking stitch.

Repeat last six rows once more.
(23 sts)

Row 57: As row 15. (21 sts)
Starting with a purl row, work three rows in stocking stitch.
Repeat last four rows five more times and then row 15 once more. (9 sts)
Starting with a purl row, work twenty-seven rows in stocking stitch.

Row 109: K1, k2tog tbl, k3, k2tog, k1. (7 sts)
Row 110: Purl.
Row 111: K1, k2tog tbl, k1, k2tog, k1. (5 sts)
Row 112: Purl.
Row 113: K1, sl1, k2tog, psso, k1. (3 sts)
Row 114: Purl.
Row 115: K3tog.
Break off yarn and fasten off.

Cast on 13 sts.
Row 1 (RS): Knit.
Row 2: Purl.

Row 3: K1, m1, k to last st, m1, k1. (15 sts)
Row 4: P1, m1, p to last st, m1, p1. (17 sts)
Row 5: K1, m1, k to end, turn, cast on 2 sts using two-needle method. (20 sts)
Row 6: P to last st, m1, p1. (21 sts)
Row 7: As row 3. (23 sts)
Row 8: Purl.
Repeat last two rows once more. (25 sts)
Row 11: K1, m1, k to end. (26 sts)
Row 12: Purl.

Repeat rows 7–8 three more times, then rows 11–12 once more. (33 sts)
Row 21: K to last st, m1, k1. (34 sts)
Starting with a purl row, work four rows in stocking stitch.
Row 26: P12, cast off 10 sts, p to end. (Two sets of 12 sts on needle)

WORK HEAD
Work head on first set of 12 sts, slipping remaining 12 sts onto stitch holder for tail.
Starting with a knit row, work twelve rows in stocking stitch.
Row 13 (RS): K to last 3 sts, k2tog, k1. (11 sts)

'Oh nergle nergle nergle!'
muttered the Soup-Dragon.

Row 14: Purl.
Repeat rows 13–14 once more.
(10 sts)
Row 17: K1, m1, k to last 3 sts,
k2tog, k1. (10 sts)
Row 18: Purl.
Row 19: As row 17. (10 sts)
Row 20: P to last st, m1, p1. (11 sts)

Cast on 16 sts using two-needle
method. (27 sts)
Repeat rows 13–14 twice more.
(25 sts)
Row 25: K1, k2tog tbl, k to last 3
sts, k2tog, k1. (23 sts)
Row 26: P1, p2tog, p to last 3 sts,
p2tog tbl, p1. (21 sts)
Row 27: As row 25. (19 sts)

Row 28: P to last 3 sts, p2tog tbl,
p1. (18 sts)
Row 29: As row 25. (16 sts)
Row 30: As row 28. (15 sts)
Row 31: As row 25. (13 sts)
Row 32: Purl.
Row 33: As row 25. (11 sts)
Row 34: As row 28. (10 sts)
Cast off and break off yarn.

The Soup-Dragon cooks soup in the volcanic
wells that lie under the pointed chimney hills
at the edge of the copper tree wood.

WORK TAIL

With RS facing, slip 12 sts from stitch holder onto needle and rejoin yarn.

Row 1 (RS): K1, k2tog tbl, k to end. (11 sts)

Row 2: P to last 3 sts, p2tog tbl, p1. (10 sts)

Row 3: As row 1. (9 sts)

Row 4 and all WS rows: Purl.

Row 5: K to last st, m1, k1. (10 sts)

Row 7: K1, k2tog tbl, k to last st, m1, k1. (10 sts)

Row 9: As row 7. (10 sts)

Row 11: As row 1. (9 sts)

Row 13: As row 1. (8 sts)

Row 14: Purl.

Starting with a knit row, work six rows in stocking stitch.

Break off yarn and slip stitches onto stitch holder.

LEFT SIDE PANEL

Cast on 13 sts.

Row 1 (WS): Purl.

Row 2: Knit.

Row 3: P1, m1, p to last st, m1, p1. (15 sts)

Row 4: K1, m1, k to last st, m1, k1. (17 sts)

Row 5: P1, m1, p to end, turn, cast on 2 sts using two-needle method. (20 sts)

Row 6: K to last st, m1, k1. (21 sts)

Row 7: As row 3. (23 sts)

Row 8: Knit.

Repeat last two rows once more. (25 sts)

Row 11: P1, m1, p to end. (26 sts)

Row 12: Knit.

Repeat rows 7–8 three more times, then rows 11–12 once more. (33 sts)

Row 21: P to last st, m1, p1. (34 sts)

Starting with a knit row, work four rows in stocking stitch.

Row 26: K12, cast off 10 sts, k to end. (Two sets of 12 sts on needle)

WORK HEAD

Work head on first set of 12 sts, slipping remaining 12 sts onto stitch holder for tail.

Starting with a purl row, work twelve rows in stocking stitch.

Row 13 (WS): P to last 3 sts, p2tog, p1. (11 sts)

Row 14: Knit.

Repeat rows 13–14 once more. (10 sts)

Row 17: P1, m1, p to last 3 sts, p2tog, p1. (10 sts)

Row 18: Knit.

Row 19: As row 17. (10 sts)

Row 20: K to last st, m1, k1. (11 sts)

Cast on 16 sts using two-needle method. (27 sts)

Repeat rows 13–14 twice more. (25 sts)

Row 25: P1, p2tog, p to last 3 sts, p2tog tbl, p1. (23 sts)

Row 26: K1, k2tog tbl, k to last 3 sts, k2tog, k1. (21 sts)

Row 27: As row 25. (19 sts)

Row 28: K to last 3 sts, k2tog, k1. (18 sts)

Row 29: As row 25. (16 sts)

Row 30: As row 28. (15 sts)

Row 31: As row 25. (13 sts)

Row 32: Knit.

Row 33: As row 25. (11 sts)

Row 34: As row 28. (10 sts)

Cast off and break off yarn.

WORK TAIL

With WS facing, slip 12 sts from stitch holder onto needle and rejoin yarn.

Row 1 (WS): P1, p2tog, p to end. (11 sts)

Row 2: K to last 3 sts, k2tog, k1. (10 sts)

Row 3: As row 1. (9 sts)

Row 4 and all WS rows: Knit.

Row 5: P to last st, m1, p1. (10 sts)

Row 7: P1, p2tog, p to last st, m1, p1. (10 sts)

Row 9: As row 7. (10 sts)

Row 11: As row 1. (9 sts)

Row 13: As row 1. (8 sts)

Row 14: Knit.

Starting with a purl row, work six rows in stocking stitch.

Break off yarn and slip stitches onto stitch holder.

NOSE PANEL

Cast on 11 sts.
Starting with a knit row, work eight rows in stocking stitch.
Row 9 (RS): K1, k2tog tbl, k5, k2tog, k1. (9 sts)
Row 10: Purl.
Row 11: K1, k2tog tbl, k3, k2tog, k1. (7 sts)
Row 12: Purl.
Row 13: K1, k2tog tbl, k1, k2tog, k1. (5 sts)
Row 14: P1, p3tog, p1. (3 sts)
Break off yarn and fasten off.

ARMS (MAKE 2)

Cast on 11 sts.
Starting with a knit row, work

fourteen rows in stocking stitch.
Shape thumb as follows:
Row 15 (RS): K5, m1, k1, m1, k5. (13 sts)
Row 16: Purl.
Row 17: K5, m1, k3, m1, k5. (15 sts)
Row 18: Purl.
Row 19: K8, turn.
Next row: P5, turn, and continue on these 5 sts only.
Starting with a knit row, work two rows in stocking stitch.
Next row: K1, k3tog, k1. (3 sts)
Break off yarn, fasten off and sew up side seam of thumb.
With RS facing and using RHN holding 3 sts, rejoin yarn and pick up 2 sts at base of thumb, then knit across 7 sts. (12 sts)
Next row: P5, p2tog, p5. (11 sts)
Starting with a knit row, work six rows in stocking stitch.
Shape top of hand as follows:
Next row: K2, k2tog, k3, k2tog, k2. (9 sts)
Next row: Purl.
Next row: K1, k3tog, k1, k3tog, k1. (5 sts)
Break off yarn, fasten off and sew up side seam of arm.

LEGS (MAKE 2 FRONT AND 2 BACK)

Cast on 13 sts.
Starting with a knit row, work nineteen rows in stocking stitch for front legs or fifteen rows for back legs.
Cast off.

FEET (MAKE 4)

Cast on 25 sts.
Row 1 (RS): Knit.
Row 2: Purl.
Shape toe as follows:
Row 3: K14, k2tog tbl, turn.
Next row: Sl1, p3, p2tog, turn.
Next row: Sl1, k3, k2tog tbl, turn.
Repeat last two rows four more times.
Next row: Sl1, p3, p2tog, turn.
Next row: Knit to end.
Next row: Purl to end.
Cast off.

MAKING UP

Sew in all loose ends. Block and press underbelly, both side panels and all four legs. Referring to the photographs as a guide throughout the making-up process, pin and sew side panels together starting at end of tail and working towards cast-off edge at head, leaving slope of nose open. Pin and sew nose panel between side panels at head.

COMPLETE TAIL

With RS facing, slip both sets of 8 sts from stitch holders onto knitting needle. (16 sts)

Row 1 (RS): K6, k2tog tbl, k2tog, k to end. (14 sts)

Row 2: Purl.

Row 3: K5, k2tog tbl, k2tog, k to end. (12 sts)

Row 4: Purl.

Row 5: K4, k2tog tbl, k2tog, k to end. (10 sts)

Row 6: P3, p2tog, p2tog tbl, p3. (8 sts)

Row 7: K2, k2tog tbl, k2tog, k to end. (6 sts)

Break off yarn and fasten off.

ATTACH UNDERBELLY

With RS facing, pin underbelly between bottom edges of side panels, starting from tail and working towards top of neck. Leave mouth section open. Sew together using mattress stitch, then insert stuffing from tail to neck, leaving head unstuffed.

WORK MOUTH

With RS facing, pick up 35 sts around top lip as follows: 13 sts along one straight side, then 9 sts along front, then 13 sts along other straight side.

Row 1 (WS): Knit.

Row 2: K to last 2 sts, turn.

Next row: Sl1, k to last 2 sts, turn.

Next row: Sl1, k to last 4 sts, turn.

Next row: Sl1, k to last 4 sts, turn.

Next row: Sl1, k to end.

Cast off.

With RS facing, pick up 33 sts around bottom lip as follows: 13 sts along one straight side, then 7 sts along front, then 13 sts along other straight side.

Row 1 (WS): Knit.

Row 2: Sl1, k to last 4 sts, turn.

Next row: Sl1, k to last 4 sts, turn.

Next row: Sl1, k to last 8 sts, turn.

Next row: Sl1, k to last 8 sts, turn.

Next row: Sl1, k to end.

Work two rows in knit.

Cast off.

With side of head facing, lay short side edge of top lip over bottom lip to create jaw. Pin and stitch into position, then repeat on other side of head. Sew in loose ends.

COMPLETE HEAD

Eyes: Position eyes evenly on nose panel seams, making sure that eye loops go straight through to WS. Sew in place on WS using yarn.

Inner mouth: To use templates provided, trace the shapes and then cut out from thin card or paper. Cut inside of mouth from black felt and tongue from pink felt. Place straight edge of tongue at centre of black felt and stitch across using pink thread. Fold black felt in half widthways and sew along fold using black thread to create a crease. Pin felt mouth to knitted mouth, aligning crease

with jaws. Starting at bottom jaw, sew lower sections together using black thread. Insert stuffing into lower jaw; do not overstuff. You may need to remove pins to do this. Insert stuffing into head, making sure that neck has enough stuffing to hold head up. Complete mouth by sewing top sections together, stuffing top lip as you go.

Feet and legs: Using mattress stitch, sew feet to bottom of legs and then sew up back seams of legs. Insert some stuffing. Using template, cut out four foot bases from thick cardboard and four from black felt. Insert cardboard into base of knitted feet, then pin felt foot bases around edges of feet. Making sure that there is enough stuffing to pad out feet, use black thread to sew felt to outer edge of each knitted foot, enclosing cardboard. Insert more stuffing into legs. Pin, then sew legs to body using mattress stitch.

Arms: Insert stuffing into arms, using knitting needle or pencil to make sure that stuffing reaches right to top and into thumb. Pin arms to body, making sure thumbs face the correct way towards each other, and then sew arms to body using mattress stitch.

Tail spike: Using template, cut tail spike from green craft foam. Use yarn needle to make hole as indicated on template.

Scales: Using photographs as a guide to shapes and a random mixture of lime-green and dark green felt and green craft foam, cut the following scales: 20 very large (3 x 2.5 cm); 20 large (2.5 x 2.5 cm); 20 medium (2 x 2 cm); 40 small (1 x 1 cm); 30 very small (0.75 x 0.75 cm). Round off the edges; slight differences will add to the effect.

Back spikes: Using the same dimensions as for the scales, cut three small, three medium and three large spikes from dark green felt. Make sure one edge is flat, though you don't need to be too precise.

Nostrils: Cut two pieces of turquoise felt, each approx. 5 x 5 mm. Round off the edges.

Attaching the pieces: Using yarn, sew tail spike to top of tail. Pin back spikes to body and head along back seam, then sew in

place using green thread. Working on one section of the dragon at a time, pin scales to body (glass-headed pins are great for this) and then stitch in place using green thread. A small back stitch at the top and/or centre of each scale will be sufficient for the body, legs and tail. For the nose, you might want to stitch around the whole scale to keep it

flat. Pin and sew on the nostrils using turquoise thread.

Spoon: Using template, cut one spoon from thick cardboard and two from brown felt. Make the felt pieces a couple of millimetres larger than the template all around. Layer cardboard between felt pieces, then stitch edges of felt together using brown thread.

LIVING CAVES AND SOUP WELL

WHAT YOU NEED

- Four cereal boxes (same size)
- Glue
- Ruler
- Saw
- Piece of wood 3 metres long, 33 mm wide and 9 mm thick
- Compass
- Pencil
- Scalpel or craft knife with sharp blade
- Two cereal boxes (any size)
- Assortment of cardboard boxes and packaging
- Three large matchboxes
- Newspapers
- Home-made glue (see page 94)
- Two plastic bottles
- Aluminium pie dishes
- Two ring pulls
- Two mini hinges
- Acrylic or poster paints in blues, pinks and white

1. To make the basic set, open out flat three of the four (same size) cereal boxes. Referring to the diagram, use glue to stick the boxes together to construct the two-sided set. Measure the length and width of the base. Using these measurements, cut the wood into four pieces. Stick these underneath the base, around the edges of the set. Measure the diagonal length of the short side of the set. Cut one more piece of wood and then glue this diagonal supporting beam on the outside of the set (see diagram).

2. For the soup well, take the fourth cereal box and in the bottom half of one side (see diagram) draw a circle with a diameter of 12 cm: use a compass with a sharp pencil as it scores the card. Divide the circle into sixteen equal parts with the pencil and ruler, and, using the scalpel or craft knife and ruler, cut along those lines. Fold the triangle sections inwards. To line the well, cut a strip of cardboard 40 cm long (stick pieces of card from cereal boxes together to reach this length) by about 6 cm wide (or the depth of the cereal box so that it fits perfectly inside). Fold the strip into a cylinder shape, put some glue on the outside and fit it into the well . Trim off any excess so that the well is flush with the surface.

3. Glue the cereal box with the well into the corner of the set.

4. To build up the walls of the set, cut off the corners of the assorted cardboard boxes, allowing a little extra card for flaps along the edges (see diagram) so as to attach them to the set. After gluing the flaps, cover the walls with about eight corners to make irregular, angular rocks.

5. On the right-hand side of the set, use more boxes and matchboxes to build up the underground Clanger world. Glue in position.

'Soup! Soup! Where's our soup?'
cried the hungry Clangers.

Inside the planet is where you will find the soup wells that lie under the pointed chimney hills at the edge of the copper tree wood. Soup wells are impenetrable to all but the Soup-Dragon, who cooks red soup, green soup and sometimes even purply-blue soup.

6. Decide where the doors will be, or refer to the photograph on page 48. To make the doorframes, twist two long thin pieces of newspaper. Dab glue on the back and stick each frame to the set. Build up the doorframes and the steps with twisted newspaper and papier-mâché (see page 94) and then cover the whole set with papier-mâché, including the back, for strength.

7. To make a soup well·turret, with the lid still in place, cut off the top 6 cm of a plastic bottle. Cover with papier-mâché. Cut out a piece of newspaper and twist it into a thin strip. Dab on a little glue and stick it around the lid to make it wider. Cover the turret with papier-mâché and leave to dry. Repeat this process to make a second turret. Once both turrets are dry, glue them to the set and cover the joins with papier-mâché.

8. Make copper trees (see page 54), then paint the set, using different shades of blues, pinks and whites as in the photograph, or use whatever colours you like.

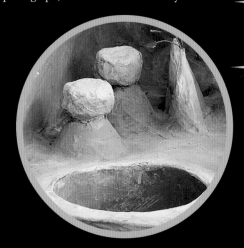

The Clangers' living caves have rather grand doors. Major Clanger and Mother Clanger occupy the sleeping cave at the top. The lower sleeping cave is for Small Clanger and Tiny Clanger.

9. For the doors, flatten the aluminium pie dishes. Cut out two small circles of card 15 mm in diameter and spray paint them silver. Glue one circle onto the centre of each door, and then glue a ring pull over the top. Glue the doors in place and finish off by gluing a mini hinge to the top of each door.

COPPER TREE

MAKING THE BASE

1. Photocopy the templates on page 90, enlarging them as stated. Carefully cut them out and place on the piece of card. Draw around, then take off the templates and cut out the shapes. Use the ruler and the back of the scalpel or craft knife to score the lines marked on the template in red. Cut the large base piece into quarters, as marked.

2. Carefully cut out the tabs and what is left of the small circle that was drawn in the centre.

3. Bend the card into a cone: make sure you leave a hole in the top for the branches to come out of. Glue the straight edges of the cone together and bend out the tabs around the bottom, where you have scored the lines, so that the cone will stand. Glue the cone to the set and then put some papier-mâché (see page 94) over the top. Repeat steps 1–3 to make more tree bases. Paint the bases with the set.

WHAT YOU NEED

- Scissors
- Thin card (or cereal box), approximately 20 × 20 cm
- Pencil
- Ruler
- Scalpel or craft knife with sharp blade
- Glue
- Reel of thin craft wire
- Gold spray paint

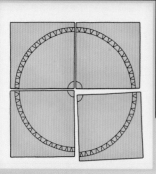
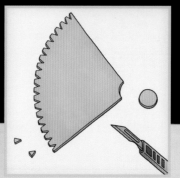
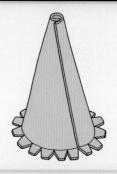

MAKING THE BRANCHES

1. Make a leaf template out of paper, either by drawing freehand or by photocopying the one on page 90. The leaves should be about 15 mm long and 10 mm wide. Place the template on the card and draw around it to make as many leaves as you need. Make sure they are all the same size as two cutouts will be sandwiched together to make one leaf: if they are different sizes you will notice. Each copper tree should have at least 5 leaves (so 10 leaf shapes to be cut in total).

2. Cut a piece of craft wire 11 cm long. Put a blob of glue on one of the leaves. Rest the wire in the glue and cover it with another leaf. Sandwich together and wipe off any excess glue. Repeat this process until you have made enough branches.

3. Spray one side of the branches with gold paint. Wait until they are dry and turn over and spray the other sides. Once they have a good coat of paint and are dry, place them in the holes of the copper tree bases.

ADULT CLANGERS

MAJOR

FINISHED SIZE
Approx. 20 cm to top of head

YARN
50-g ball (1 per Clanger) of
Rowan Pure Wool DK in Tea
Rose 025

MATERIALS
- Pair of 2.75-mm knitting
  needles
- Yarn or tapestry needle and
  safety pins for sewing up
- Toy stuffing
- Pins
- Oddment of pink felt for
  nose, ears and hands
- Sewing needle and thread to
  match each colour of felt
- Oddment of black felt for
  eyes and feet
- Thin card
- Oddment of felt for hair
  in colour of your choice
- Oddment of deep blue
  felt for Mother's bow
- Sheet of felt for tunic,
  approx. 23 × 30 cm, in
  black (Grannie), red
  (Mother) and beige (Major)
- Small amount of metallic
  thread or 4-ply yarn in silver
  (Grannie) and gold (Mother)
  for tunic embroidery
For Major's outfit only:
- Gold craft paint
- Small paintbrush
- Small amount of 0.3-mm
  gold craft wire for sewing
  tunic
- 20 cm of 1-mm brass
  craft wire for collar
- Long-nose pliers

TENSION
Approx. 32 sts and
45 rows to 10 cm over
stocking stitch using
2.75-mm needles

ABBREVIATIONS
See page 81

TEMPLATES
See pages 82–83

HEAD, BODY AND LEGS

Cast on 10 sts.

Row 1 (RS): Knit.

Row 2: Purl.

Repeat last two rows once more.

Row 5: K1, m1, k to last st, m1, k1. (12 sts)

Row 6: Purl.

Repeat last two rows until there are 30 sts, ending with a purl row.

Row 25: As row 5. (32 sts)

Row 26: P1, m1, p to last st, m1, p1. (34 sts)

Repeat last two rows until there are 44 sts, ending with a knit row.

Row 32: Purl.

SHAPE BACK OF HEAD

Next row (RS): K1, m1, k to last 2 sts, turn.

Next row: Sl1, p to last 2 sts, turn.

Next row: Sl1, k to last 4 sts, turn.

Next row: Sl1, p to last 4 sts, turn.

Continue in this way, working 2 sts less on each row until 'sl1, p to last 16 sts, turn' has been worked.

Next row: Sl1, k to last st, m1, k1. (46 sts)

Next row: Purl to end.

Continue working in stocking stitch, increasing 1 st as set in row 5 at each end of every knit row until there are 62 sts, ending with a knit row.

SHAPE ARMHOLES

Next row (WS): P12, cast off next 6 sts, p26 (include st used in cast-off), cast off next 6 sts, p to end.

Next row: K1, m1, k11, turn, cast on 6 sts, turn, k26, turn, cast on 6 sts, turn, k to last st, m1, k1. (64 sts)

Next row: Purl to end.

Continue working in stocking stitch, increasing 1 st as set in row 5 at each end of every knit row until there are 68 sts.

Work next seventeen rows straight, ending with a purl row.

SHAPE LOWER BACK AND LEGS

Row 1 (RS): K16, k2tog, k6, k2tog, k16, k2tog tbl, k6, k2tog tbl, k to end. (64 sts)

Row 2 and all WS rows: Purl.

Row 3: K16, k2tog, k5, k2tog, k14, k2tog tbl, k5, k2tog tbl, k to end. (60 sts)

Row 5: K16, k2tog, k4, k2tog, k12, k2tog tbl, k4, k2tog tbl, k to end. (56 sts)

Row 7: K16, k2tog, k3, k2tog, k10, k2tog tbl, k3, k2tog tbl, k to end. (52 sts)

Row 9: Cast off 5 sts, k16 (include st used in cast-off), cast off 10 sts, k to end.

Row 10: Cast off 5 sts, p16 (include st used in cast-off), turn. Starting with a knit row, work six rows in stocking stitch on this set of 16 sts.

Cast off and break off yarn. With wrong side facing, rejoin yarn to remaining 16 sts and, starting with a purl row, work seven rows in stocking stitch. Cast off.

ARMS (MAKE 2)

Cast on 12 sts.
Row 1 (RS): Knit.
Row 2: Purl.
Row 3: K1, m1, k to last st, m1, k1. (14 sts)

Starting with a purl row, work five rows in stocking stitch.
Row 9: As row 3. (16 sts)
Starting with a purl row, work five rows in stocking stitch. Cast off.

OUTER EARS (MAKE 2)

Cast on 5 sts.
Row 1 (WS): Purl.
Row 2: K1, m1, k3, m1, k1. (7 sts)
Row 3: Purl.
Row 4: K1, m1, k5, m1, k1. (9 sts)
Row 5: Purl.
Row 6: K1, m1, k7, m1, k1. (11 sts)
Starting with a purl row, work three rows in stocking stitch.
Row 10: K1, k2tog tbl, k5, k2tog, k1. (9 sts)
Row 11: P1, p2tog, p3, p2tog tbl, p1. (7 sts)
Row 12: K1, k2tog tbl, k1, k2tog, k1. (5 sts)
Row 13: P1, p3tog, p1. (3 sts)
Cast off.

MAKING UP

Sew in all loose ends. Gently press arms and ears, and the outer edges of body to stop the edges from curling: this will help with the sewing up. Fold body in half, wrong sides together, and pin the edges at regular intervals to keep them even. With right side facing, use mattress stitch to sew from the bottom seam towards the nose. Starting from the cast-off edge, sew up the legs using a long enough tail of yarn so that you can sew the bottom seam once the Clanger has been stuffed. Insert stuffing through the open bottom seam, using a small amount to start with so that you do not overstuff the nose. Once stuffed, sew up the bottom seam. Fold one arm in half, wrong sides together. With right side facing, use mattress stitch to sew up the cast-on edge and side seam of arm. Repeat for the second arm, then stuff both firmly and sew securely to the armholes.

FEATURES

To use the templates provided, trace the shapes and then cut them out from thin card or paper. Refer to the photographs as a guide for positioning the features and sew them in place using thread to match the felt colour.

Eyes: Cut two small circles of black felt, then pin and stitch to head.

Nose: Cut a small circle of pink felt, then stitch into position.

Ears: Using template and pink felt, cut two inner ears and stitch to wrong side of knitted outer ears. Pin and stitch ears to head, leaving enough space between the ears for the hair.

Hands: Using template and pink felt, cut two hands, then pin and stitch to bottom of arms.

Feet: Using template, cut four feet from black felt and two more

'Nothing is proper here!' complained Mother Clanger. 'This is the only blue-string pudding bowl I have and this soup-stirrer is almost worn out and there are only six mugs to drink soup out of and…' She went on complaining.

from card. Trim the card pieces so that they are slightly smaller than the felt pieces. Sandwich each card piece between two black felt pieces and sew around the edges. Once both feet have been completed, pin and stitch to bottom of legs.

Hair: Using template, cut hair from desired colour of felt, then pin and stitch into position between ears.

OUTFITS

To use the templates provided, trace the shapes and cut them out from thin card or paper. Refer to the photographs as a guide for making up the outfits.

Grannie: Using templates, cut the pieces for the tunic from black felt. Use metallic silver thread or 4-ply yarn to work a running stitch around the outer edges of each felt piece. Sew the tunic pieces together using thread to match the felt, checking regularly to make sure that the tunic will fit onto the body and the pieces are not too close together or too far apart.

Mother: Make the tunic in the same way as Grannie's, but use red felt and gold metallic thread or 4-ply yarn. To make the bow for her hair, cut a rectangle of deep blue felt, approx. 2.5 × 3 cm. Pinch the felt at the centre to form a concertina shape, allowing the edges to fan out. Using blue thread, sew along the centre to secure. Position the bow on top of the head between the ears and sew to the hair.

Major: Using templates, cut the pieces for the tunic from beige felt. Cut out two large C shapes from beige felt and sew onto the centre of the front and back tunic panels using beige thread. Lay all the tunic pieces on top of a sheet of newspaper to protect the surface you are working on and paint the pieces with gold paint. Leave to dry (approx. 1 hour). If required, apply another coat of gold for a stronger colour and leave to dry again. Sew the tunic pieces together using gold wire, checking regularly to make sure that the tunic will fit onto the body and the pieces are not too close together or too far apart. The tunic hangs on a brass wire collar around the Major's neck. Bend the brass wire and place it around the Major's neck to check that it fits, trimming if necessary. Grip one end of the wire with long-nose pliers and wind the wire around to form a loop. Repeat at the other end of the wire. Check once again that the collar fits, then bend the ends slightly downwards to an angle of approx. 45 degrees. Place the collar around the Major's neck, then sew the front and back of the tunic to the collar using gold wire.

GRANNIE

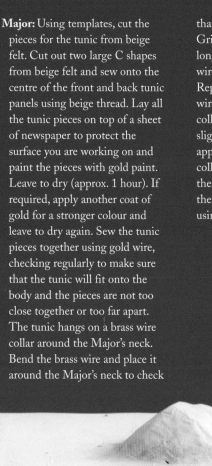

ROCKET

10

WHAT YOU NEED

- 1.5-litre plastic bottle
- Ruler
- Scissors
- Compass (or bowl)
- Thin card (or cereal box)
- Scalpel or craft knife with sharp blade
- Glue
- Plastic cup
- Pack of craft foam
- Wooden barbeque skewers
- Pliers/side cutters
- Hole punch
- Pack of lolly sticks (at least 25)
- Four ballpoint pens
- Two thick pens
- Cotton reel
- Gold spray paint

TO MAKE THE ROCKET

1. First cut 5 cm off the bottom of the plastic bottle. Using the compass or by laying a bowl onto the card, draw a circle approximately 18 cm in diameter, cut it out then cut it in half. Take one half and twist it into a cone shape. Bend the cone shape around the cut off end of the bottle and glue in place. Trim any excess, then glue the edges of the cone together. Glue the plastic cup to the other end of the bottle.

2. Cut out four strips of craft foam, each measuring 1 cm wide and long enough to go around the bottle. Glue one strip around the cone/bottle join and another around the bottle 3 cm below. Glue another strip around the cup/bottle join. Put the last strip to one side.

3. Cut sixteen lengths of skewers, each measuring 5 cm. Referring to the illustration right, glue eight skewer pieces (spaced evenly) around the two strips of craft foam at the top of the rocket. Make sure that the bottoms of the skewers are flush with the bottom of the lower strip of craft foam. Glue the remaining eight lengths next to each of the skewers already in place. Glue the last piece of craft foam around the top of the skewers.

4. Using the hole punch, cut at least twenty-four circles out of the craft foam to decorate the rocket.

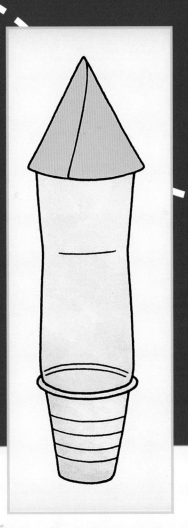

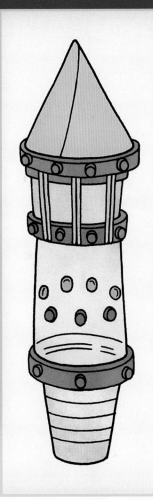

5...4...3...2...

TO MAKE THE LAUNCH PAD

1. Work out how big the rocket launch pad should be. Measure the diameter of the rocket and add 1 cm. For instance, if it is 7.5 cm. add 1 cm, making it 8.5 cm. Cut down eight lolly sticks to this length. These will form the top and bottom pieces of the four sides of the cradle.

2. Use eight full-length lolly sticks for the diagonals of the four sides of the cradle. For each side, take two short and two full length lolly sticks, lay them down on a table with the shorter lengths at the top and bottom and the full-length sticks placed diagonally. Glue them together. Repeat this four times to make all four sides of the cradle.

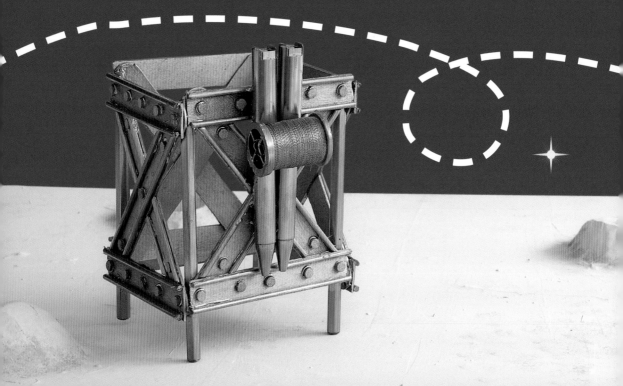

3. Take two sides of the cradle and glue two ballpoint pens (at the top and bottom of each pen) to each piece (see illustration). Make sure that the ends stick out the same length at the bottom, around 2.5 cm.

4. Take one of the sides with the biros attached and one without and glue together at a 45-degree angle. (See illustration of finished cradle.)

5. Take the other piece with ballpoint pens attached and glue this, again at a 45-degree angle, to form the third side. This will be opposite the other side of the cradle with pens. Make sure the cradle stands level.

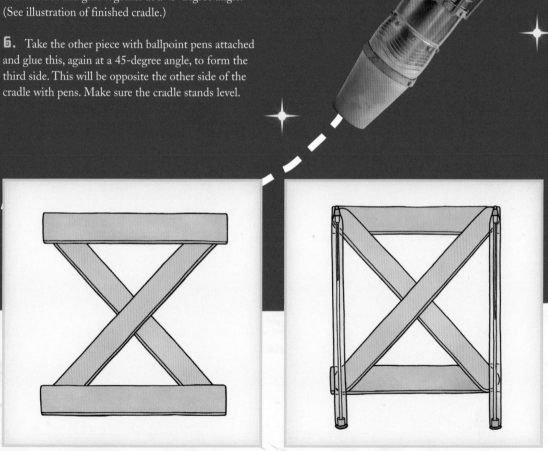

'Marvellous! Marvellous!'
Major Clanger cried.
'We Clangers must build our own
space rocket and fly in it to that
distant golden planet.'

7. Finally glue the last side of the cradle in place.

8. Now for the detailing, which adds depth to the model. Using the photograph of the final cradle as reference, cut down wooden skewers to size and glue them onto the edges of the lolly sticks.

9. Take the two thick pens and glue them next to each other on one side of the rocket launch pad.

10. Glue the cotton reel onto the pens, sideways on in the centre.

11. Using the hole punch, cut at least seventy circles out of the craft foam to decorate the rocket launch pad.

12. Spray both parts of the model gold (following the instructions on the can). It is better to do a few thin coats rather than one thick coat as the paint may run. Wait for the paint to dry in between each coat.

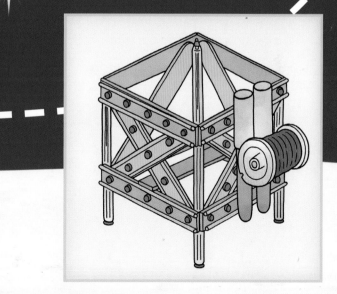

IRON CHICKEN

The Iron Chicken has an inner and outer body, and lots of other parts. This makes it a more advanced project. However, if you follow the steps carefully, you can reconstruct this feisty bird – just as the Clangers did!

The wings, body decoration, tail and feet on our chicken are made from lollypop sticks. You could use cardboard if you prefer and make the holes with a hole punch. If you do use lollypop sticks, you may need to sand down any rough edges with fine-grain sandpaper.

If you wanted to make a simpler version, you could try using whatever you've got at home to make the head and body. Cut out feather shapes using our templates (see pages 92–93) and glue them on before painting your chicken silver.

The Iron Chicken lives on her cosy comfy spiky nest of old scrap-iron and bits of machinery which she has gathered up in her travels.

TO MAKE THE WINGS

1. Photocopy the templates on page 92, enlarging them as stated. Carefully cut them out and place on the lolly sticks or card. Draw around, then take off the templates and cut out the shapes. Either cut out the middle sections of the wing pieces, or leave the shapes as they are.

2. Lay all the wing pieces out in front of you. You should have 18 altogether – two base pieces and 16 wing pieces. Glue the split peas and lentils onto the pieces, to make rivets and bolts, as shown in the diagram and the photograph.

3. Remember you need to make one wing for the left side and one for the right. Glue the wing pieces on to the wing base, starting from the top down, using the photograph below and the diagram as a guide.

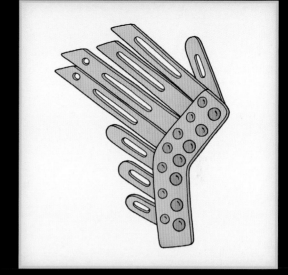

TO MAKE THE BODY

1. Photocopy the body templates on pages 91-92, enlarging them as stated. Carefully cut them out and place on the piece of card. Draw around, then take off the templates and cut out the shapes. Use the ruler and the back of the scalpel or craft knife to score the lines marked on the template in red. You should have ten body pieces altogether.

2. Take the six internal body pieces, and using the diagram (right) for reference, make the inner body. Fold the tab on piece 4 down and glue to piece 3 as shown. Repeat this process with piece 5 and 6, and glue to the middle and bottom of piece 3.

3. Next slide piece 2 (the middle support) onto pieces 4 and 5, as shown. Fold the tab on piece 6 and glue to piece 2 (see diagram). Lastly, fold the tabs on pieces 4 and 5, then match up with piece 1 and glue into place.

4. To attach the top of the body, dab a small amount of glue along the top outer edges of sections 1–3 of the inner body. Then match up the folds of the top section and press down gently to stick.

5. To attach the bottom part of the body, dab a small amount of glue along the bottom outer edges of sections 1–3. Then match up the folds of the bottom section and press gently.

6. Now add the side panels. Bend along the fold lines to form the shape of the body. Dab a little glue onto the tabs of the top and bottom pieces and attach one side panel. Repeat for the other side.

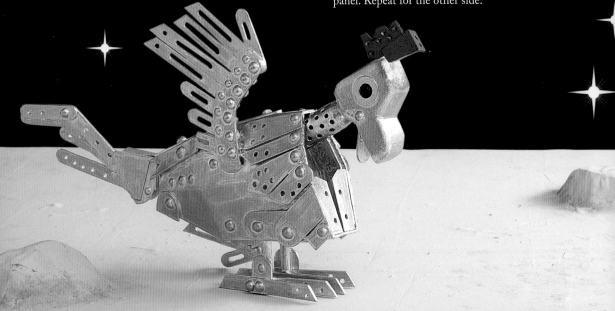

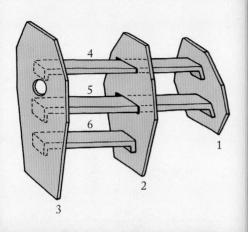

4
5
6
1
2
3

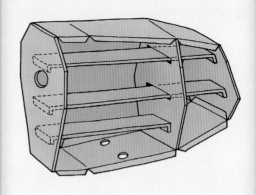

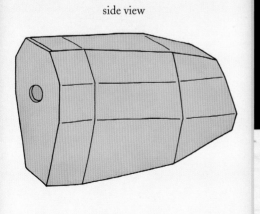

side view

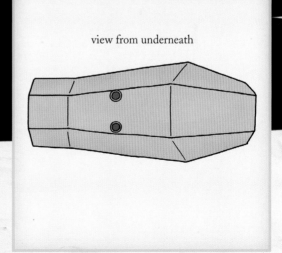

view from underneath

TO MAKE THE HEAD

1. Photocopy the head, comb and beak templates on page 93, enlarging them as stated. Carefully cut them out and place on the piece of card. Draw around, then take off the templates and cut out the shapes. Don't forget to transfer the star markings onto your head pieces. Use the ruler and the back of the scalpel or craft knife to score the lines marked on the template in red.

2. Fold along all the tabs and fold lines of piece B. Check that this long piece of cardboard fits around the side peices of the head. Then matching up the stars, and starting at the back of the head, glue the tabs into position around one of the side pieces. The tabs can sit on the outside. Leave to dry.

3. Place a blob of Blu-Tack inside the head, at the top, using the diagram as a guide. This is for the neck support to sit in. Tightly roll a piece of thin card around the pencil and use sticky tape to secure. Insert the pencil up through the neck opening of the head so the point of the pencil sits in the Blu-Tack.

4. Attach the other side of the head – again sticking the tabs to the outside of the side piece, so you can press down more easily. Once the head is dry, glue another head panel to each side to cover up any tabs. Then glue the washer and split pea into position for the eye, using the diagram as a guide. Fold the tab on the beak piece, and glue into position as shown. Next glue the comb into position on the top of the head.

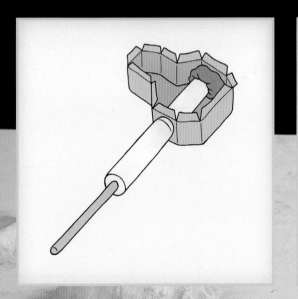

5. To make the neck, punch small holes in another piece of thin card, and roll this around the pencil to form an outer neck layer. Use sticky tape to secure.

6. Lastly, glue the base of the neck into position on the front section of the body. Push the pencil through the hole and glue into place. Cut down the length of the pencil if necessary, and use sticky tape to secure until the glue is dry.

TO MAKE THE FEET AND LEGS

1. Photocopy the feet templates on page 93, enlarging them as stated. Carefully cut them out and place on the lolly sticks or card. Draw around, then take off the templates and cut out the shapes. Either cut out the middle sections of the feet pieces, or leave the shapes as they are. You should have four pieces for each foot.

2. Using the diagram as a guide, glue the pieces to the doweling, to make two feet. Add your split peas and lentils for bolts and rivets, as shown. Once the glue is dry, make sure the legs will fit through the cut-out circles in the body. Enlarge your holes slightly if necessary. Add glue to the top of the legs and insert into the holes, making sure the feet are the right way round, then press firmly and hold for the glue to bond.

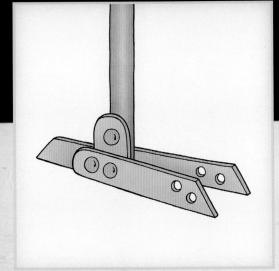

TO MAKE THE TAIL

1. Photocopy the tail templates on page 93, enlarging them as stated. Carefully cut them out and place on the lolly sticks or card. Draw around, then take off the templates and cut out the shapes. Either cut out the middle sections of the pieces, or leave the shapes as they are. You should have seven pieces altogether.

2. Now glue pieces 1–4 (the tail feathers) together, using diagram as guide. Leave to dry.

3. Glue on pieces 5 and 6, using the diagram as a guide. Leave to dry.

4. Now attach the tail to the body. Bend the sides of piece 7 upwards, and add a dab of glue to the middle section. Stick this onto the centre of body piece 1 (the chicken's bottom). Glue the tail feather section inside the centre of piece 7. Add a dab of glue to the insides of piece 7 and squeeze together to hold the tail in place.

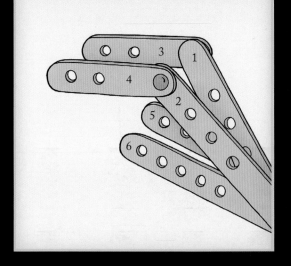

FINISHING THE CHICKEN

1. Photocopy the decorative body parts templates on page 92, enlarging them as stated. Carefully cut them out and place on the lolly sticks or card. Draw around, then take off the templates and cut out the shapes. Either cut out the middle sections of the pieces, or leave the shapes as they are. Glue the split peas and lentils onto the pieces, to make rivets and bolts, as shown in the diagram (left). You should have twenty pieces altogether.

2. Now attach the decorative body parts to each side of the main body, using the diagram as a guide.

3. Using the photographs as a guide, glue the wings to the sides of the body – leave to dry.

4. Spray the chicken silver (following the instructions on the can). It is better to do a few thin coats rather than one thick coat as the paint may run. Wait for the paint to dry in between each coat. Paint the chicken's crest with bronze acrylic paint. Paint the eye black. If you decided not to cut out all the small holes in the wings, tail, feet and body pieces, you can add these on with black paint if you like.

KNITTING BASICS

WORKING FROM A PATTERN

Before starting any pattern, always read it through. This will give you an idea of how the design is structured and the techniques that are involved. Each pattern includes the following basic elements:

MATERIALS

This section gives a list of materials required, including the amount of yarn, the sizes of needles and extras.

ABBREVIATIONS

Knitting instructions are normally given in an abbreviated form, which saves valuable space. In this book the abbreviations are listed on page 81.

PROJECT INSTRUCTIONS

Before starting to knit, read the instructions carefully to understand the abbreviations used, how the design is structured and in which order each piece is worked. However, there may be some parts of the pattern that only become clear when you are knitting them, so do not assume that you are failing to understand or that the pattern is wrong.

TENSION AND SELECTING CORRECT NEEDLE SIZE

Tension can differ quite dramatically between knitters. This is because of the way that the needles and the yarn are held. So if your tension does not match that stated in the pattern, you should change your needle size following this simple rule:

- If your knitting is too loose, your tension will read that you have fewer stitches and rows than the given tension, and you will need to change to a smaller needle to make the stitch size smaller.
- If your knitting is too tight, your tension will read that you have more stitches and rows than the given tension, and you will need to change to a thicker needle to make the stitch size bigger.

MAKING UP

The making up section in each project will tell you how to join the knitted pieces together. Always follow the recommended sequence.

KNITTING A TENSION SWATCH

No matter how annoying it seems to have to spend time knitting a tension swatch before you start, please do take the time, as it will not be wasted.

Use the same needles, yarn and stitch pattern as those that will be used for the main work and knit a sample at least 12.5 cm square. Smooth out the finished piece on a flat surface, but do not stretch it.

To check the stitch tension, place a ruler horizontally on the sample, measure 10 cm across and mark with a pin at each end. Count the number of stitches between the pins. To check the row tension, place a ruler vertically on the sample, measure 10 cm and mark with pins. Count the number of rows between the pins. If the number of stitches and rows is greater then specified in the pattern, make a new swatch using larger needles; if it is less, make a new swatch using smaller needles.

MAKING A SLIP KNOT

A slip knot is the basis of all casting-on techniques and is therefore the starting point for almost everything you do in knitting.

1. Wind the yarn around two fingers twice, as shown. Insert a knitting needle through the first (front) strand and under the second (back) one.

2. Using the needle, pull the back strand through the front one to form a loop. Holding the loose ends of the yarn with your left hand, pull the needle upwards, thus tightening the knot.

CASTING ON

Casting on is the term used for making a row of stitches to be used as a foundation for your knitting.

1. Place the slip knot on the needle, leaving a long tail, and hold the needle in your right hand.

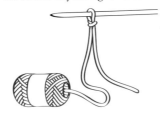

2. Wind the loose end of the yarn around your left thumb from front to back. Place the ball end of the yarn over your left forefinger.

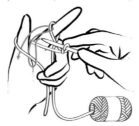

3. *Insert the point of the needle under the loop on your thumb. With your left index finger, take the ball end of the yarn over the point of the needle.

4. Draw a loop of yarn through to form the first stitch. Remove your left thumb from the yarn. Pull the loose end to secure the stitch. Repeat from * until the required number of stitches has been cast on.

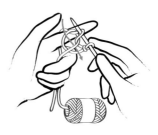

THE BASIC STITCHES

The knit and purl stitches form the basis of all knitted fabrics. The knit stitch is the easiest to learn. Once you have mastered this, you can move on to the purl stitch. Projects in this book use stocking stitch, which is made by alternating rows of knit and purl.

KNIT STITCH

1. Hold the needle with the cast-on stitches in your left hand, with the loose yarn at the back of the work. Insert the right-hand needle from left to right through the front of the first stitch on the left-hand needle.

2. Wrap the yarn from left to right over the point of the right-hand needle.

3. Draw a loop of yarn through the stitch, thus forming a new stitch on the right-hand needle.

4. Slip the original stitch off the left-hand needle, keeping the new stitch on the right-hand needle. To knit a row, repeat steps 1 to 4 until all the stitches have been transferred from the left-hand needle to the right-hand needle.

PURL STITCH

1. Hold the needle with the stitches in your left hand, with the loose yarn at the front of the work. Insert the right-hand needle from right to left into the front of the first stitch on the left-hand needle.

2. Wrap the yarn from right to left, up and over the point of the right-hand needle.

3. Draw a loop of yarn through the stitch, thus forming a new stitch on the right-hand needle.

4. Slip the original stitch off the left-hand needle, keeping the new stitch on the right-hand needle. To purl a row, repeat steps 1–4 until all the stitches have been transferred from the left-hand needle to the right-hand needle.

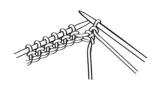

INCREASING AND DECREASING

Many projects will require some shaping. This is achieved by increasing or decreasing the number of stitches you are working.

INCREASING

The simplest method of increasing one stitch is to work into the front and back of the same stitch. On a knit row, knit into the front of the stitch to be increased into; then, before slipping it off the needle, place the right-hand needle behind the left-hand one and knit again into the back of the same stitch (inc). Slip the original stitch off the left-hand needle.

On a purl row, purl into the front of the stitch to be increased into; then, before slipping it off the needle, purl again into the back of it. Slip the original stitch off the left-hand needle.

DECREASING

The simplest method of decreasing one stitch is to work two stitches together.

On a knit row, insert the right-hand needle from left to right through two stitches instead of one, then knit them together as one stitch. This is called knit two together (k2tog). On a purl row, insert the right-hand needle from right to left through two stitches instead of one, then purl them together as one stitch. This is called purl two together (p2tog).

CASTING OFF

This is the most commonly used method of securing stitches once you have finished a piece of knitting. The cast-off edge should have the same 'give' or elasticity as the fabric, and you should cast off in the stitch used for the main fabric unless the pattern directs otherwise.

KNITWISE

Knit two stitches. * Using the point of the left-hand needle, lift the first stitch on the right-hand needle over the second, then drop it off the needle. Knit the next stitch and repeat from * until all stitches have been worked off the left-hand needle and only one stitch remains on the right-hand needle. Cut the yarn, leaving enough to sew in the end, thread the end through the stitch, then slip it off the needle. Draw up the yarn firmly to fasten off.

PURLWISE

Purl two stitches. * Using the point of the left-hand needle, lift the first stitch on the right-hand needle over the second and drop it off the needle. Purl the next stitch and repeat from * until all the stitches have been worked off the left-hand needle and only one stitch remains on the right-hand needle. Secure the last stitch as described in casting off knitwise.

FINISHING TECHNIQUES

You may have finished knitting but there is one crucial step still to come, the sewing up of the seams. It is tempting to start this as soon as you cast off the last stitch, but a word of caution – make sure that you have good light and plenty of time to complete the task.

MATTRESS STITCH (SIDE EDGES)

This stitch makes an almost invisible seam stocking stitch. Thread a tapestry needle with yarn and position the pieces side by side, right sides up.

1. Working from the bottom and leaving a 10cm tail of yarn, take the needle through the edge loop of the first row on the right-hand piece, then through the same loop on the left-hand piece. Then go back across to the right-hand piece and pass the needle under the first two of the horizontal bars that divide the columns of stitches above the cast on edge.

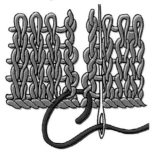

2. Take the needle to across to the left-hand piece and pass it under the first two of the horizontal bars that divide the columns of stitches. Take the needle to across to the right-hand piece, insert the needle down through the fabric where it last emerged and pass it under the next two of the horizontal bars that divide the columns of stitches above the cast on. Repeat step 2, zigzagging between the pieces and going under two bars each time. After every few stitches, pull gently to close the seam.

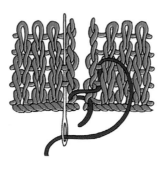

MATTRESS STITCH (TOP AND BOTTOM EDGES)

Thread a tapestry needle with yarn and position the pieces top and bottom, right sides up.

Working left to right, come up from back to front through the centre of first stitch on the right edge of the seam and leave a 10cm tail of yarn. Take the needle across to the top piece, pass the needle under the two loops of the stitch above, then go down again, through the fabric, where the needle emerged on the lower piece. Bring it out through the middle of the next stitch to the left and repeat stitch by stitch across the row.

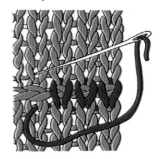

ABBREVIATIONS

This is a list of all the abbreviations used in the knitting instructions in this book. Refer to this as you are working your way through the pattern.

INSERTING STUFFING

As with all soft toys, how you stuff your doll will directly affect the finished appearance. It is important to stuff firmly, but without stretching the knitting out of place. Always stuff the extremities, such as the legs and arms, first and mould the pieces into shape as you go along. The amount of stuffing needed for each doll depends on the knitting tension and individual taste.

approx	approximately
alt	alternate
beg	beginning
cm	centimetre(s)
dec	decrease
g	gram(s)
inc	increase
k	knit
k2tog	knit two stitches together
k3tog	knit three stitches together
k2tog tbl	knit two stitches together through back of loops
LHN	left-hand needle
m1	make 1 stitch by picking up strand between stitch just worked and next stitch on left-hand needle and working through back loop

mm	millimetre(s)
p	purl
p2tog	purl two stitches together
p3tog	purl three stitches together
p2tog tbl	purl two stitches together through back of loops
psso	pass slipped stitch over
rep	repeat
RHN	right-hand needle
RS	right side
sl1	slip 1 stitch
st(s)	stitch(es)
tbl	through back of loop(s)
tog	together
WS	wrong side

TEMPLATES

CLANGER TEMPLATES

Enlarge by 200%

Adult Hair
Cut 1

Small Hair
Cut 1

Tiny Hair
Cut 1

Adult Foot
Cut 2

Small Foot
Cut 2

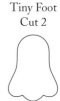
Tiny Foot
Cut 2

Adult Ear
Cut 2

Small Ear
Cut 2

Tiny Ear
Cut 2

Adult Hand
Cut 2

Small Hand
Cut 2

Tiny Hand
Cut 2

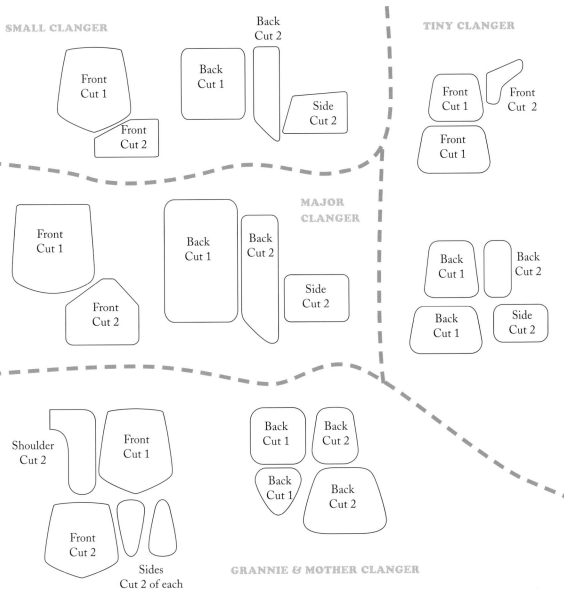

SMALL CLANGER

Front Cut 1

Front Cut 2

Back Cut 1

Back Cut 2

Side Cut 2

TINY CLANGER

Front Cut 1

Front Cut 2

Front Cut 1

Back Cut 1

Back Cut 2

Back Cut 1

Side Cut 2

MAJOR CLANGER

Front Cut 1

Front Cut 2

Back Cut 1

Back Cut 2

Side Cut 2

Shoulder Cut 2

Front Cut 1

Front Cut 2

Sides Cut 2 of each

Back Cut 1

Back Cut 2

Back Cut 1

Back Cut 2

GRANNIE & MOTHER CLANGER

BOAT TEMPLATES

Enlarge by 200%

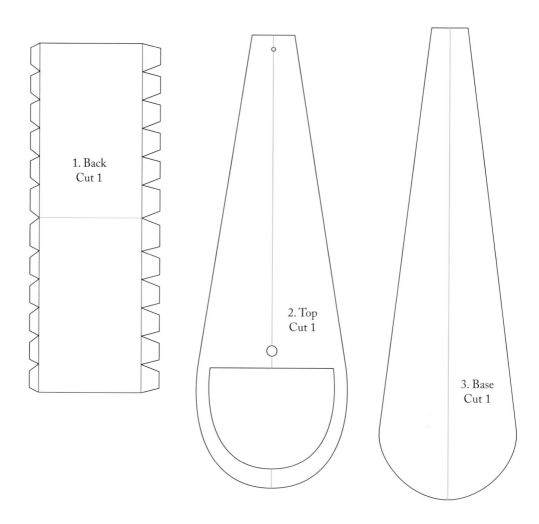

1. Back
Cut 1

2. Top
Cut 1

3. Base
Cut 1

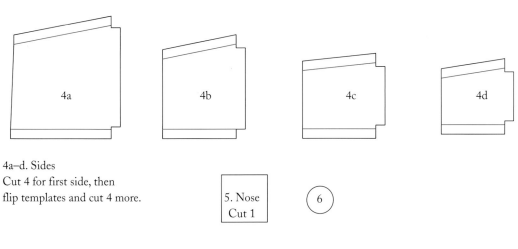

4a–d. Sides
Cut 4 for first side, then
flip templates and cut 4 more.

5. Nose
Cut 1

6

MUSIC WHEEL

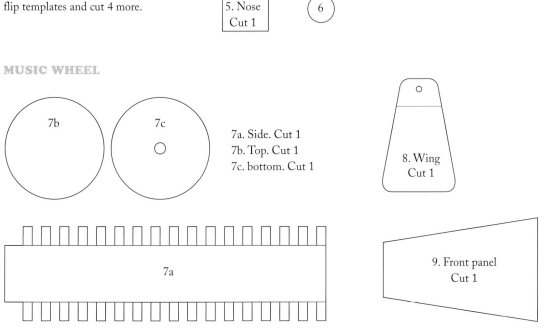

7a. Side. Cut 1
7b. Top. Cut 1
7c. bottom. Cut 1

8. Wing
Cut 1

9. Front panel
Cut 1

SEE SAW TEMPLATES

Actual size

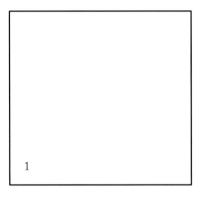

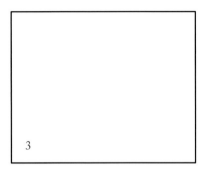

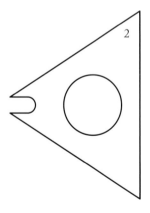

1. Base. Cut 1
2. Sides. Cut 2
3. Seat. Cut 2

PIN TREE TEMPLATES

Enlarge by 200%

1. Outer tree. Cut 2
2. Inner tree. Cut 1
3. Supports. Cut 2
4. Pincushions. Cut 5

4

1

2

3

FROGLET & TOP HAT TEMPLATES

Enlarge all templates by 200% except the Froglet's foot, which is actual size

FROGLETS

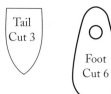

Tail
Cut 3

Foot
Cut 6

TOP HAT

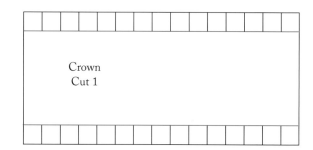

Crown
Cut 1

TOP HAT – BOW

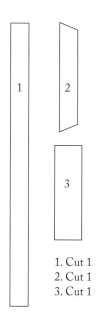

1

2

3

1. Cut 1
2. Cut 1
3. Cut 1

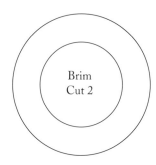

Brim
Cut 2

Top
Cut 2

SOUP DRAGON TEMPLATES

Actual size

Tail spike
Cut 1

Foot Base
Cut 2

Spoon
Cut 1

Mouth
Cut 1

Tongue
Cut 1

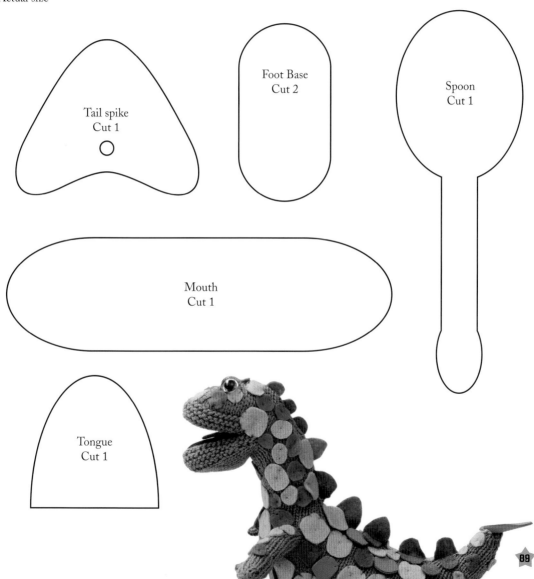

COPPER TREE TEMPLATES

Enlarge by 150%

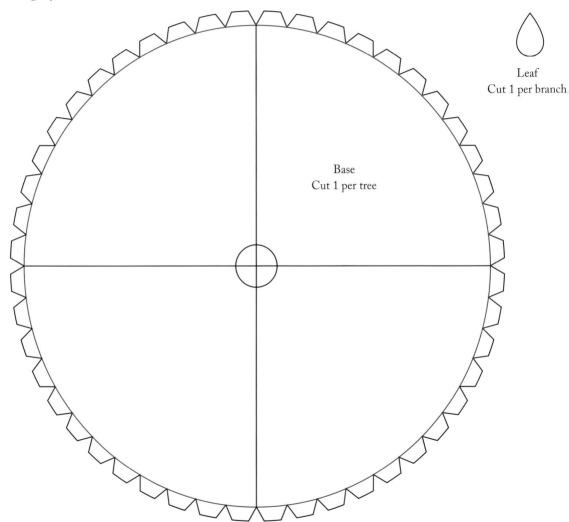

Leaf
Cut 1 per branch

Base
Cut 1 per tree

IRON CHICKEN TEMPLATES

Enlarge by 150%

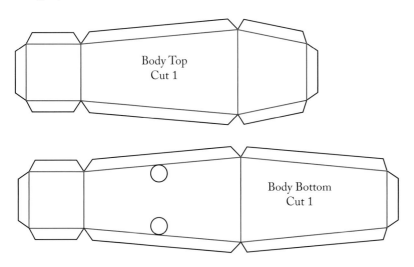

Body Top
Cut 1

Body Bottom
Cut 1

1

2

3

1-6. Internal body pieces.
Cut 1 of each.

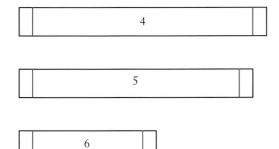

4

5

6

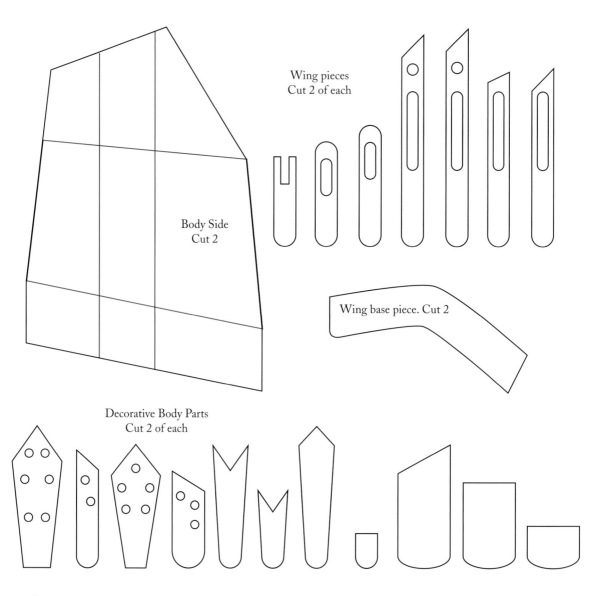

Wing pieces
Cut 2 of each

Body Side
Cut 2

Wing base piece. Cut 2

Decorative Body Parts
Cut 2 of each

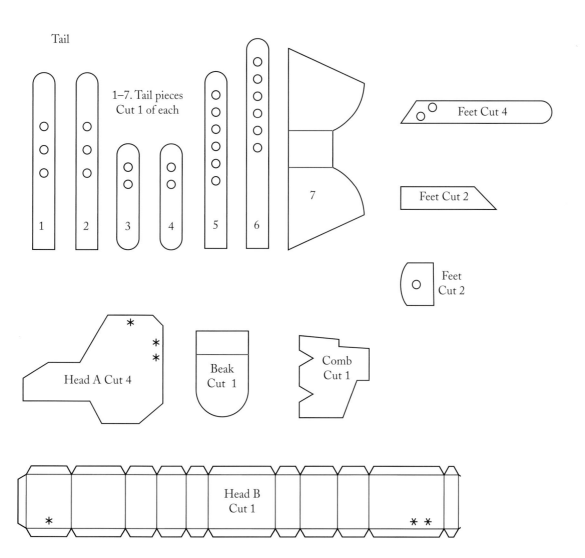

Tail

1–7. Tail pieces
Cut 1 of each

1

2

3

4

5

6

7

Feet Cut 4

Feet Cut 2

Feet
Cut 2

*

*
*

Head A Cut 4

Beak
Cut 1

Comb
Cut 1

Head B
Cut 1

*

* *

PRACTICAL ADVICE & SAFETY TIPS

The Clangers love to build things out of the bits and pieces that they have found lying around their planet. In this book we have tried to make sure that all the materials for the projects are easy to find at home or to buy inexpensively at your local craft store. If you can't find exactly the right materials, it doesn't matter! Use whatever you can find and be creative! Try and be inventive – use cereal boxes, yoghurts pots, and any other empty packaging you have around the house. Perhaps you want your Froglets to be bigger, or your rocket to be smaller – that's fine!

HOME-MADE GLUE

Makes just under 1 litre of glue. Fill a saucepan with half a litre of water and bring to the boil, then allow to simmer. Sieve four heaped dessert spoons of plain or self-raising white flour and add this to the simmering water. Stir continuously until it thickens to a paste. Turn off the heat and let the glue cool down until it is ready to use.

PAPIER MÂCHÉ

Tear or cut newspaper into squares. Depending on the surface you want to cover, the squares should be between 2 × 2 cm to 15 × 15 cm. For detailed and rounded shapes use smaller pieces. For flat, large areas use bigger pieces. Follow the instruction for making home-made glue. Dip the squares of newspaper into the home-made glue and remove any excess glue. Lay the saturated pieces of newspaper over the area you wish to cover, smoothing with your fingertips. Overlap each piece, covering the required area. Once the papier mâché has dried, you may wish to do a second layer, either for strength or to neaten the effect.

CRAFT SUPPLIERS

Use materials that you have around the house, or visit these suppliers:

Hobbycraft
From Aberdeen to Bournemouth, Hobbycraft have stores up and down the country, or you can buy online.
www.hobbycraft.co.uk

Rowan Yarns
Many thanks to Rowan Yarns for supplying yarn for the knitted projects.
www.knitrowan.com

PUBLISHER'S ACKNOWLEDGEMENTS

This book would not have been possible without the encouragement and support of Peter and Joan Firmin. We cannot thank them enough for their kindness and generosity in sharing their world of the Clangers with us. Our thanks also to Daniel Postgate. The Clangers ran for three series that were repeated for many years and the 26 episodes are widely available today on DVD.

Peter and Joan's grand-daughter, set designer Ruth Herbert (www.ruthherbert.com), is an absolute star and her talented recreation of the Clangers' planet is truly amazing. Carol Meldrum (www.beatknit.com), knitter extraordinaire, has risen to the challenge of recreating all of the characters for us.

Here at Collins & Brown, Amy Christian, Laura Russell, Nina Sharman, Gemma Wilson, Matt Johnstone and Holly Jolliffe have all played a vital role in making these characters and sets come alive on the page.

Our biggest thanks are to all of the Clangers and the Soup-Dragon, Froglets and the Iron Chicken for showing us what really lives in space and beyond…

Join our crafting community at LoveCrafts – we look forward to meeting you!

First published in the United Kingdom in 2012 by Collins & Brown
1 Gower Street
London WC1E 6HD

An imprint of Pavilion Books Company Ltd

Design and text copyright © Collins & Brown 2012

All characters based on the *Clangers* films made by Oliver Postgate and Peter Firmin, as Smallfilms, for the BBC.

ISBN 978-1-90844-905-4

A CIP catalogue for this book is available from the British Library.

10 9 8 7 6 5 4 3 2

Reproduction by Rival Colour Ltd, UK
Printed and bound by
GPS Group Ltd, Slovenia

This book can be ordered direct from the publisher at www.pavilionbooks.com

13

14

15

16

17

18

THE SOUP-
DRAGON
MAKES YOU
A BOWL OF
SOUP – RUN
FORWARD 2
SQUARES

JUMP INTO THE
FROGLETS' HAT,
THEN APPEAR
MAGICALLY 4
SQUARES
FORWARD